9/04   B
55

D0108748

LEE GLICKSTEIN

BE
HEARD
NOW!

· · · · · · · · · · · · · · · · · · ·

Tap into Your

Inner Speaker and

Communicate with Ease

BROADWAY BOOKS · NEW YORK

BROADWAY

BE HEARD NOW! Copyright © 1998 by Lee Glickstein. All
rights reserved. Printed in the United States of America. No
part of this book may be reproduced or transmitted in any form
or by any means, electronic or mechanical, including photo-
copying, recording, or by any information storage and retrieval
system, without written permission from the publisher. For information, address Broadway Books, a division of Bantam Doubleday Dell Publishing Group, Inc., 1540 Broadway, New York,
NY 10036.

Broadway Books titles may be purchased for business or promo-
tional use or for special sales. For information, please write to:
Special Markets Department, Bantam Doubleday Dell Publishing Group, Inc., 1540 Broadway, New York, NY 10036.

BROADWAY BOOKS and its logo, a letter B bisected on the diag-
onal, are trademarks of Broadway Books, a division of Bantam
Doubleday Dell Publishing Group, Inc.

Speaking Circles® and its logo is a registered trade-
mark of Lee Glickstein and may not be used without his express
written permission.

Library of Congress Cataloging-in-Publication Data

Glickstein, Lee.
  Be heard now! : tap into your inner speaker and communicate with ease / by Lee Glickstein. — 1st ed.
     p.   cm.
  ISBN 0-7679-0260-2 (hardcover)
  1. Public speaking.   I. Title.
PN 4121.G56   1998
808.5′1—dc21   98-24252
                                                    CIP

FIRST EDITION

Designed by Pei Koay

98 99 00 01 02 10 9 8 7 6 5 4 3 2 1

BE
HEARD
NOW!

For Morris Glickstein,

Grandfather of Speaking Circles,

and the man who made this work

both necessary and possible.

ACKNOWLEDGMENTS

Heartfelt thanks to Carol Costello and Grant Flint for their vital help in preparing the manuscript.

Chapter 5

CONNECTION IS EVERYTHING: DROPPING THE
BARRIER BETWEEN SPEAKER AND AUDIENCE   **92**

Chapter 6

VIBRANT VULNERABILITY:
THE WISDOM OF NOT KNOWING   **111**

Chapter 7

EMBRACING FEAR: SHED "THE SHAKES"
AND END YOUR STAGE FRIGHT FOREVER   **127**

Chapter 3

BEING YOURSELF:

THE KEY TO COMPELLING RAPT ATTENTION   **43**

Chapter 4

LISTENING WITH THE HEART:

LETTING OTHERS "BE HEARD NOW!"   **65**

CONTENTS

. . . .

One day I found the magic key. After suffering from a terrible fear of public speaking for forty-eight years, I reversed it in myself—transformed the energy of fear into *magnetism*.

And I found a way to coach others to dramatically turn *their* fear of public speaking around—to instantly convert a history of stage fright into a natural sense of stage *right*.

At the heart of such fears is a performance-oriented approach to speaking to groups. We feel we must perform. Not be ourselves. We must put on an act, an exhibition, something for the stage.

When we shift from performance to relationship-oriented speaking, relating one-to-one, friendly, personal, real, speaking conversationally to each one in the audience, a miracle happens—the fear is gone! We never again have to be afraid in front of groups.

Whatever your level of education, speaking experience, or lack of it, when you move fully into relationship-orientation with your audience—speaking to them personally, one by

one—you become a "born-again speaker" with infinite resources.

Whether you are a professional speaker dedicated to realizing your highest potential, an occasional speaker, or a non-
speaker with debilitating stage fright, this book will show you
easily how to drop false stage techniques, worries, and unnatural obstacles. It will instead put you in touch with your infinitely creative source, your "Inner Speaker," the real you, the
warm, human, natural you, the one who has waited so long to
speak.

Even if you don't plan to speak in public, but suffer a debilitating shyness in groups or with individuals, this book addresses the core of your dilemma, and the ideas here apply
to you.

Be Heard Now! puts to rest the conventional "wisdom" that
only those born with a silver tongue—or nerves of steel—
can speak with golden results. For beginner and experienced
speaker alike, it will help you access your deepest creativity
and find a new sense of purpose in the world—your Inner
Speaker knows the higher calling of your heart and soul.

Here you will learn things that no traditional speaking class
tries to teach. Relationship-orientation to groups cannot be
taught by technique, but it can be *caught* by a deep awareness
of the realities presented.

You will soon understand exactly why speaking out is a
problem for most people. And you will see your way clear to
tapping into your Inner Speaker—which has remained as
fresh and fertile as the day you locked it away.

The reality is that you were a born speaker. You "goo-
gooed" and "gah-gahed" with the best of them. You expressed
yourself effortlessly and creatively in play and pain—until
you were told by people you trusted that you didn't know
how to speak.

This book will help you discover your authentic truth. Believe it or not, this truth, simply expressed to a group, results in uniquely eloquent style, just-right content, and poignant, humorous storytelling. Even your deepest and most valid fears cannot stop this wonderful process from happening if you apply the ideas and guidelines that follow.

If you are weary of thinking big and feeling small, if you agree with writer and speaker Marianne Williamson that "There's nothing enlightened about shrinking so that other people won't feel insecure around you," come join me in the great adventure of speaking with ease.

Lee Glickstein, October 1998

Chapter 1

FROM AGONY TO ECSTASY:

TAPPING INTO YOUR OWN

NATURAL POWER

◉

Would you like to transform your agony over speaking in public to ecstasy, no more waiting?

Speaking without fear is your birthright!

Picture this:

> "I physically shake in terror and am unable to communicate a point of view."
>
> •
>
> "I am petrified, waiting for the audience to expect me to do badly."
>
> •
>
> "I'm a polished, professional speaker, but I have a deeper message hidden away and I feel I'm turning my back on it."

• You are asked to present a toast at your best friend's wedding. No problem. You'll look into the happy couple's eyes and tell them what's in your heart.

• Tomorrow morning you're giving a three-minute pep talk to your sales team. You take five minutes to consider what you want to cover. Now you can't wait to get at 'em.

• Tonight you are speaking to 150 people. Instead of being

paralyzed with fear and anxiety, uncertain about the outcome—or compulsively overpreparing and rehearsing
every word of your talk—you are looking forward to the
evening!

Do these scenarios sound impossible, or at least unrealistic?
No longer. This is the essence of a new way to communicate
based on relaxed, natural, authentic human connections, and
on accessing your genuine passion.

Speaking from our heart lets us compel rapt attention
every time we speak. Even inexperienced speakers with severe stage fright can gain heartfelt support and immediate
trust in sales presentations and classrooms, at dinner tables, in
corporate training—while giving a toast at a wedding or a
keynote to ten thousand.

Speaking can be fun! Easy, delightful, electric, cathartic,
and fulfilling.

You deserve *not* to have stage fright. And if you are already
a polished speaker, you deserve to learn how to go *beyond*
polish.

You will never again have to memorize a speech.

You can be a free, warm, happy speaker and captivate your
audience every time.

Everyone can give a talk without fear. Most people were
taught to fear groups as a child. That dread will now disappear.

Some of you have already suffered terribly in front of
groups. Maybe you will recognize yourself in these real-life
quotes:

• "I'm an introvert, not a performer. In college speech
class I threw up after every speech."
• "When I speak to even a few people, fear of saying the
wrong thing and looking stupid just overwhelms me."

- "I'm so painfully self-conscious, my throat tightens up and I have trouble breathing."
- "I have difficulty finishing even one sentence, let alone getting across what's in my heart."

Some of you suffer from a different anguish:

- "Shyness isn't my problem, nor do I have stage fright. But I hide behind a rhetorical speaking style, like a politician. I don't really reveal my heart. I have a deeper message hidden away, but I feel like I'm running scared."

There is a new, easier way to *enjoy* talking to three people or to three thousand.

This book tells how to do this. Simply, quickly. You can now be happy in front of people. You can now be yourself. In this book, you will discover:

- How to get past public speaking myths: public speaking is not about performance. It is about expression of our authentic selves. Stage fright is not to be conquered and overcome. It must be honored and moved through. Critical feedback does not spur improvement. Positive feedback nurtures growth.
- How to defuse your Inner Critic.
- How to quickly be yourself—the key to compelling *rapt* attention.
- Why humor is not about making people laugh. Humor is about *letting* people laugh!
- Why being real is mesmerizing.
- How to find your natural speaking style—one that has a deep impact on people.
- How to *listen* while you speak. Why good listeners are good speakers.
- How to have instant rapport—the four basic steps to connect with any audience.

- How to go from being charisma-impaired to *vibrantly vul-nerable.*
- How to turn nervousness into——*nirvana!*
- How to quickly and easily prepare a talk that opens minds and reaches hearts.

From Charisma-Impaired to Vibrantly Vulnerable

I grew up "charisma-impaired" and developed these principles and practices from my own desperate need to overcome the world's worst stage fright.

The very first public talk of my life was a disaster. It was my bar mitzvah speech. Bar mitzvah is the ceremony at which a Jewish boy comes of age——but at thirteen, puberty for me was still just a rumor. I uttered the traditional opening line, spoken by Jewish boys throughout the ages: "Today I am a man." Only instead of the assertive adult voice I was trying for, the line came out in a squeaky soprano!

It brought down the house, and I was so embarrassed that I didn't speak again in public for twenty-five years.

In 1974 I moved to California and became deeply involved in the human potential movement. Many of us "potential humans" were exploring our inner selves with Werner Erhard, Ram Dass, encounter groups, sensitivity training, and every other psychospiritual fad that came down the pike.

I avidly aspired to "become a person," though to paraphrase a Lily Tomlin line, I later wondered if maybe I should have been more specific.

But I was also exploring stand-up comedy and public speaking. Putting my feet directly into the fire seemed the only way I'd ever get through stage fright, a fright that felt more like winged bats than "butterflies in my stomach."

More than a decade before Tony Robbins had his followers walking on hot coals, I trod scorching stages as a way of dealing with my excruciating shyness. It helped, but not enough: I was still shy, but now I could almost survive being shy in front of *many* people instead of just two or three. I transformed my hidden insecurity into public insecurity. My bats were beginning to fly in formation. My performance hysteria had subsided into anxiety. Clearly, there was more to learn.

Unlike some aspiring speakers, I was constitutionally incapable of covering up my nervousness and insecurity with the techniques or posturing that serve as a crutch for "Outer Speakers," my term for those who hide their true selves, who speak to the audience, not to individuals—who put on an external show as camouflage to disguise the true self, the wonderful Inner Speaker.

Frankly, such tricks made me *more* self-conscious and uncomfortable as I struggled with acting "lessons" and gimmicks billed as "surefire" audience turn-ons. My apparent liability, however, held the key to everything I now know about public presentation.

I experimented with processes that might help me—and would later help the clients I coached in presentation skills. One day I asked myself what would happen if I *didn't* try to cover up my discomfort, *didn't* pretend I wasn't tongue-tied, *didn't* talk faster and faster to avoid the silences, *didn't* memorize every word for fear of drawing a blank?

I had no way of knowing whether this utter *lack* of presentation would work. At first I found the thought of a more natural approach *un*natural! But I wanted to test out my theories (or hunches, really) to see if they worked.

I decided to get a few people together—and have each of us take a turn standing in front of the group, being exactly who we were in that moment. We could do whatever we wanted for five minutes—talk, sing, recite poetry, or just stand in silence.

We didn't have to cover up our nervousness; it was okay to be nervous, or sad, or silent, or joyful, or outraged. And no matter how we felt or what we did, the others would give us their full attention and support.

Our only ground rules: we would explore how it felt to stay connected with people in the audience, *and accept the unconditional support and positive regard of the group.* When we were finished, everyone would *give only positive feedback* about what they felt when we were in front of the room.

We would bask in a completely safe environment—in that rare condition of being fully seen and heard by other people. Our only job would be to explore how it felt to receive that much attention and acknowledgment. And to let in as much of it as we could.

It sounded almost too good to be true, so I put together some groups and tried it out.

The Speaking Circles Start to Turn

. . . .

At first, some people resisted all the positive attention and support. They complained that being supported no matter what we did—and hearing only what people liked about our presentations—"wasn't fair," or "wasn't real." But we decided to put aside that resistance and try it anyway—to see whether a more natural, personal approach to speaking in public in a supportive environment works.

The results were astonishing. People blossomed in miraculous ways when they felt fully seen and heard—and when they acted exactly the way they felt. Again and again, we saw that a few minutes of focused support could dissolve a life-time of holding back with groups, and that those who were already good at receiving support could become even more comfortable with themselves, and therefore even more magnetic, more charismatic.

Those who had been nearly paralyzed by the fear of speaking in public began to relax into a lovely, confident presence. People who had adopted "stagy" or "slick" personas became genuine and vulnerable. People who had never felt that anything they said would be valued began to see that their voices could influence others.

Even *I* was able to move from charisma-impaired to vibrantly vulnerable. It was a completely uplifting and enriching experience that produced startling breakthroughs.

It seemed like magic. We had stumbled onto a way for anyone to be charismatic, because it turned out that the most compelling thing any of us could do in front of the group was to be real—to be authentically, genuinely ourselves. That was the thing that inspired trust—and attracted people like a magnet!

Old Myths, New Realities
. . . .

To be HEARD now, you have to be HERE now.

That brings a whole new dimension to what happens when one person speaks and other people listen.

When most of us hear the words "public speaking," we tend to believe certain myths about how we should and shouldn't communicate. But the reality of our attention-challenged society forces us to change how we interact with one another—and to think about public speaking on five fronts:

1. *OLD MYTH: Public speaking is about mastering PERFOR-MANCE and winning the audience over with style and technique.*
NEW REALITY: Public speaking is about EXPRESSION of our authentic selves.

When speaking is a performance, the audience is watching a performer or actor—not necessarily a person who is relating from his or her authentic self. An invisible curtain always keeps this performer at a certain distance from the audience. Performance requires a script, rehearsals, and lots of effort. It traps the performer into a prescribed set of "Do"s and "Don't"s. He can only go so far toward his own truth, or toward the audience.

Twenty years ago I performed stand-up comedy. I wasn't bad. I memorized my jokes and recited them word for word. If people laughed, I would remember my next line. If they didn't, I would be lost for the evening, which in most cases was mercifully only five minutes.

One night I was doing well. They were with me. Then I was exposed as not being with *them*. A lamp fell near the back of the room. There was a boom, and a light flared out. But I could not afford to register any of it. I was on to my next joke. They rightfully shut me out the rest of the way.

Ten years later I found out how *not* to be a performer, yet make it work to be me in a big way. When I speak in front of groups, I now find that I can be entertaining, en-lightening, magnetic, and humorous, but with no fixed agenda or strings to pull.

Magic happens when we approach speaking from the perspective of expressing ourselves, not performing. When speaking is the natural expression of what we be-lieve and live, then our audience is spending time with a human being who is telling his or her own truth. Our passion becomes infectious. We can relax, and thus people listening to us can relax.

One speaker said it was like being an artist: "The air space is my canvas and I am the brush."

The new reality turns automated public speakers into authentic speakers, and practitioners list authenticity first among all the benefits of performance-oriented speaking.

• "Practicing connecting with my audiences helped break me out of a formula style of speaking into a much more lively, natural, and personally enjoyable way of presenting my ideas," said Dr. Neil Fiore, a psychologist and author who lectures across the country.

• "When I'm being most myself on stage, I can actually feel the audience being touched by me," said a corporate trainer.

• "Exploring expression in front of a group allows me to connect my heart to my theories, and to discover why the things I speak and write about are important to me," a novelist said.

• "What a relief to find that I could be more effective by speaking to the audience in my natural style, directly from my heart and gut, rather than according to the teachings of traditional public speaking classes," said Hermann Maynard, a business consultant.

Authenticity is being touted as one of the most effective leadership tools around. In an age of cynicism and distrust, it is one of the few things that inspire people to action. To get authentic commitment from people, we need to inspire them with genuine passion. What we say doesn't count for much if people don't believe us, or if they don't think that we believe ourselves. Today, enlightened business leaders build trust and get results by revealing their authentic selves and setting an inspired example. If I were putting millions into a project, I would want to look into my associates' eyes and see someone authentic at home in there. Wouldn't you?

2. OLD MYTH: *Stage fright must be conquered and overcome.*
NEW REALITY: *Stage fright must be honored and moved through.*

"Stage fright" is not a syndrome reserved for actors and entertainers. Any time self-consciousness impedes communication, whether one-on-one or with a group, there is a degree of stage fright present. This trait seems to be built into the human condition.

The way to move through stage fright organically, to dissolve it rather than merely mask it, is *to stand before a supportive group and let ourselves feel the fear.* We may even want to talk about it.

This accomplishes two things. First, we are no longer fighting the fear. Whenever we resist something we are feeling, it becomes like a beach ball that we're trying to hold under water.

We can push it down again and again, but the minute we relax our grip, it springs to the surface and makes a big splash. When we stop resisting the fear, we stop giving it power. We stop making it strong by providing it with something to push against.

Second, when we allow ourselves to feel our fear in front of a supportive group who would never do all the terrible things we're (consciously or unconsciously) afraid they are going to do to us, we start breaking down our belief that there is something to fear.

When a group beams appreciative attention on someone with stage fright, *the fear usually melts away*—and is often replaced by an absolute joy and a new expressiveness that comes as much from relief as it does from receiving the support. When the fear honestly disappears, rather than just getting covered up, we can move more deeply into our own wisdom and reach out more directly to the audience—even an audience in the "real world" that has not agreed to be unconditionally supportive.

Here is what two speakers had to say about stage fright:

• "I've been speaking to large groups for fifteen years and have always had a big fear of drawing a blank. With support, I've discovered that when I don't know what to say next, I can just take a few seconds 'in the void.' Something always comes—and when I see myself on videotape, that silence looks fine. As a result, I have created a whole new, and more honest, relationship with my audiences."

• "I started out terrified to show my real self. It's a natural fear for those of us who have suffered some crushing event. But when I talked about what had 'crushed' me to a supportive group who just listened and didn't try to 'fix' me, I got through it in just a few minutes. Now I can open up and talk about what *excites* me in life."

We will explore the concept of embracing stage fright in greater detail in chapter 7.

3. **OLD MYTH:** *Public speaking is a task with defined parameters.*

NEW REALITY: *Public speaking is an art with infinite possibilities.*

The traditional motivation for improving our communication in front of groups is professional development, whether in the service of becoming a paid speaker or a more effective business leader.

"I wanted to polish my speaking skills to promote the psychoeducational program I've developed as a family therapist," said Tom Handlan. "I came to speaking class to work on presentations, like I was bringing in a car to get a good paint job to make it look shiny and slick."

What Tom found, in contrast to his desire to "polish my speaking skills," was a class that asked the question: "Where is your passion?"

"It wasn't about the outside but about looking inward," he says. "It's finding the spark that gets me going in the morning, finding what drives me through the day, and what helps me to move beyond obstacles and detours to focus on the goal."

Finding the "Inner Speaker"—our real self, warm, intimate, honest, the voice we use to speak truly to our loved ones—is a satisfying and transforming process that helps us know ourselves better, work through difficulties we have connecting with others, get clearer on what we believe, and find a stronger voice to express those beliefs in all areas of our lives.

Here are some views of the place speaking holds in our lives:

• "Speaking has become for me a transformational experience. Every time I get up on stage I learn more about myself. I grow, and I'm pushed to say what I believe. We all have a particular knowledge, and I believe we're put on earth to speak that truth."

• "Expressing myself on stage with support allows me to synthesize my ideas, thoughts, and experiences until sparks fly and I am amazed at what comes out of my mouth. I am learning what my unique gift is by sharing it. This clarity gives me more self-confidence in everything I do, not just speaking."

4. *OLD MYTH: Critical feedback spurs improvement.*
NEW REALITY: Positive feedback nurtures growth.

Too many speaking careers are sabotaged in the early stages by the "friendly fire" of well-meaning suggestions from friends and associates in the guise of "advice," "helpful criticism," and "the honest truth"—"truths" like:

- "I counted five 'um's in your talk."
- "You speak too fast."
- "You seemed nervous."
- "You might try walking across the stage and gesturing like so to drive home that point."

Speakers at any stage of professional development make quantum leaps in self-expression when they get generous amounts of support and appreciation. People flourish when we invite only positive feedback. There is no need to be shamed in public in order to know what you want to correct—and critical "corrections" are not only paralyzing, but often inaccurate.

5. *OLD MYTH: Humor is about* making *people laugh.*
NEW REALITY: Humor is about letting *people laugh.*

As discussed in greater detail in chapter 8, healthy and effective humor comes out of sharing an awareness of our common humanity—our frailties, the tensions in our relationships, the chatter of our minds. Laughter flows when we remember that the human mind is God's little practical joke, and when we share the embarrassment of being human—together. Humor that is mean-spirited, deprecating, or manipulative isn't funny for very long. But humor that is inclusive and kind-hearted will stand the test of time.

Authentic speaking allows the natural humorist and storyteller within us to emerge:

· "People laugh at the most unexpected places when I'm telling stories about my life! I'm at my funniest when I'm really not trying to be funny but am just having a good time recounting an incident."

· "As a humorist, when I share my humanity and emotions I am gently massaging the listeners' pain until it turns to pleasure, like when someone tenderly pushes and rubs the crick in your back."

· "As we get older and wiser, we find out more about who we've always been. It's sort of like a banana, peeling off some of those defense mechanisms and expressing what's underneath. Drama is about peeling the onion; comedy is about peeling the banana."

The Four Great Truths of All Good Communication

Before we delve into the "how-to's," let us look at an overview of public speaking in the light of our new approach.

1. The most compelling thing we can do is to be real—to be authentically, genuinely ourselves—and no one can do that as well as we can.

Everyone has a story to tell, a unique message to deliver, and a special voice in which to express it. Our presence speaks more loudly than anything we say. If we are at ease with ourselves, people know it and can relax with us.

The more comfortable we are, the more eloquent and compelling we become.

"When I'm standing up there feeling inspired by the glow in my listeners' faces, those are the exact times I'm told *I* am inspiring," says a secretary.

Authentic speakers don't use formal "styles" or "public speaking techniques"—because these tend to mask our authentic selves and are not particularly compelling. The best technique is *no* technique.

2. A deep, powerful presence and relaxed self-expression emerge naturally when we are fully seen and heard in a safe, supportive environment.

When we can be completely free from any fear of criticism, rejection, or reprisal, our most authentic selves emerge naturally.

As this essence is nurtured over time with positive feedback, the layers of defenses fall away. The more we are *ourselves,* the more the audience can be *themselves,* which makes the room even safer, which lets us be more ourselves, and so on into a powerful upward spiral.

"I used to love my pajama parties," a corporate trainer told me. They were safe, cozy gatherings where we girls told the truth and no one put on airs. Thirty years later, I lead what I think of as 'pajama circles,' and I am in heaven!"

3. Connection is everything.

As we speak, we "listen" to our audience, and return again and again to our common humanity and heart-and-soul connection.

The key to instant rapport is making others feel fully seen and heard in our presence. When we listen to others, they listen to *us.* When we honor people with our full attention and regard, they listen to what we say, whether we are speaking to one person or ten thousand people.

4. The key to connecting with any audience is not knowing how to give to them—but knowing how to receive support from them.

It's not what we put out, it's what we allow our audience to give, that determines our relationship with them.

These four elements of effective public speaking—being ourselves, creating a safe environment, connecting with the audience, and receiving support—all work together and strengthen one another. When we do any one of them, the other three are enhanced.

"Transformational Speaking": Genuine, Natural Power

The *Be Heard Now!* principles developed out of the experience of two thousand Speaking Circles. This greenhouse environment gave birth to "transformational speaking." When you make speaking a relationship event (person-to-person, one-on-one, intimate, real, warm) rather than a performance event (distant, staged, manipulating), you have achieved the easy miracle—you have become a "transformational speaker." You are changed. Your audience is changed. You and your listeners are one, transported to a deeper, higher level of rapport.

Transformational speaking is speaking from the heart directly to one member of the audience at a time. It transforms fear of speaking to joy of speaking. It transforms a performance into an intimate conversation. It transforms an Outer Speaker (external, distant, manipulative) into an Inner Speaker (warm, personal, intimate).

People everywhere are realizing that those who can stand before others in a genuine way, being themselves in all their glory and vulnerability, can get more done and produce better results in all areas of their lives.

"Transformational speaking is on the cutting edge of what's going on in this country in business," says Doug Krug, a trainer of corporate leaders and co-author of *Enlightened Leadership: Getting to the Heart of Change*. He writes:

> It's clear that what we've been doing just isn't working. We've been trying to deal with the surface stuff, not the real issues, which are people issues! People want to get real and authentic, and business leaders are beginning to see that they have to get real with their potential customers and clients—and with their employees.

And it's true. People want to do business with those who can look them in the eye and connect deeply. They recognize slickness. They want to be dealt with honestly and given a chance to express themselves and have their best evoked. They want leaders in whom they have faith, leaders who have, as Doug Krug calls them, "the 'soft skills' of support, listening, connection, and authenticity."

Consultant and professional speaker Chuck Moyer, president of TrendPower, adds, "The key to balance and success in business and relationships in the twenty-first century will be a keen awareness of and attention to the basic human need of human beings to be fully seen and fully heard *exactly as we are*."

Until recently, we might not have used these terms to describe successful business relationships. Today, the same values described in this book are on the cutting edge of American corporate culture.

The Ten Great Benefits of Transformational Speaking
. . . .

1. Confidence. We learn how to move through fears easily and quickly, and become more at ease with ourselves and others. Even if we are nervous, we don't panic.

2. Authenticity. We become more natural and real, and we open into a genuine, heartfelt connection with our audience.

3. Spontaneity. "Thinking on our feet" becomes second nature. A natural humor starts to emerge that relaxes listeners and makes them more receptive. We move from stage fright and compulsive overpreparation to relaxed spontaneity.

"It's like I can't do anything wrong up there when I'm in the flow. Everything works because I say it does," says a salesman.

4. Clarity. We speak simply, clearly, from the heart. Because we are calm and clear, we influence our listeners in a natural way.

5. Self-expression. As we open ourselves to the dance of giving and receiving, we naturally become more self-expressive.

"Since I began telling my audiences that I was motivated to get into financial planning by my dad's failure to create a secure future for my mom and myself, I've become aware of deeper levels of commitment to my clients," says Chuck Root. And this inspires more of his listeners to *become* clients.

6. Instant rapport. We connect with people on a human level and honor their essence, so *they want us to succeed.*

7. Better listening. We learn to listen to people, even

while we are speaking. This carries over into all aspects of our lives, enriching both business and personal relationships.

8. *Being heard.* When we listen to people and let them support us, they listen to us!

9. *Charisma.* We learn to find and honor our own unique charisma, which lets us speak to groups as naturally as we would to friends over coffee. That's an irresistible force—one-to-one or in a huge auditorium.

10. *Personal growth.* We develop higher self-esteem, enjoy better relationships, become more productive, and find a deeper appreciation of others.

Eve Hinman is an engineer who specializes in the design of terrorist-resistant buildings. She recently did a briefing in Washington about a report she wrote for a high-risk government agency moving into a new federal facility not designed to resist explosions.

I played it in my usual low-key manner. One guy in the meeting said, "Have you conferred with [a certain consulting firm that happened to be my previous employer] for your study? I've read some very excellent reports from them on the Oklahoma City bombing." I responded, "Well, I wrote those reports."

Before my practice in transformational speaking, I would have gotten self-conscious about it. It would have made me feel uncomfortable to have that kind of positive attention paid to me. Now my ego enjoyed it. It feels natural to be an expert and have that expertise confirmed publicly. I chatted with him afterwards and made a new professional friend.

Transformational speaking represents not only a new way of speaking, but a new way of living, relating, and doing business.

Who Are the Transformational Speakers?

People of many different ages, economic circumstances, walks of life, and outlooks become transformational speakers.

Studies show that speaking in public is the number one fear among Americans, outranking even the fear of death! In the ten years I've coached public speaking, I have heard this fear expressed many ways. Here are three situations in which these fears typically show up.

• "I'm fine one-to-one, with colleagues I see every day or even people from out of town. But put me in front of three or more people, and I freeze up. It's as if somebody reached in and cauterized my brain cells."

• "I make my living training departments within corporations to communicate better, and I do a good job—but I have to be hyperprepared and it's agony! I have to know everything I'm going to say a week before I say it, and rehearse endlessly. I just want to be relaxed and comfortable with those people. I want to be spontaneous."

• "I hold back at church or PTA because I'm not quite sure what I want to say—and I'm afraid people won't listen anyway. When I do have to stand up and give a committee report, I just go as fast as I can to get it over with."

Which Kind of Speaker Are You?

• Are you confident addressing a group when you know exactly what you are going to say, but lose presence when you need to be spontaneous?

• Do you run a meeting or training session with great spontaneity and excitement, but go stiff and dull when asked to present a prepared talk?

• Does the prospect of standing in front of any group fill you with feelings of shyness, discomfort, anxiety, or dread—*even though you know in your heart you have a contribution to make?*

• Are you already a good speaker who could use some leading-edge coaching to take you over the top?

I have tested the methods in this book with more than three thousand groups over nine years: CEOs, salespeople, entrepreneurs, trainers, schoolchildren, artists and writers, storytellers, community leaders, health care professionals, people in career transition, and others from every walk of life, including professional speakers.

These methods can turn almost anyone into a relaxed, compelling speaker who actually enjoys being in front of groups. And who can communicate a clear message with high impact—just by being themselves.

Confidence about public speaking carries over into all aspects of personal and professional life. Transformational speaking takes you to the next level, whether you aspire to be a five-figure speaker like management consultant Tom Peters, address your staff for five minutes with your head held high, or inspire your friends over lunch.

"Mealtime is a fun time to play with this communication approach," Elizabeth, a wife and mother, told me. "After I get someone's attention and before I ask them to 'please pass the salt,' I make soft, deliberate eye contact for two to three seconds. Then I stay connected for a couple of seconds after my 'thank you.' There is a wonderful shift in the sense of attention around the dinner table. It brings the family together."

Practicing These Principles

. . . .

You can practice this natural way of speaking in a conference room or in your own living room. The final chapter will give you all the tools you need to set up your own peer support Speaking Circle. *Thousands of people have moved from agony in front of groups to ecstasy in weeks, sometimes in minutes, in these sessions.*

An international community of transformational speakers has emerged from the thousands of sessions done to date. Our farthest-flung circle, made up of recovering stammerers in Ireland, has let it be known that they welcome visitors from any other part of the world, whether stutterers or not, to sit in and participate in their circle.

"We stammerers are the only Irishmen who have not kissed the Blarney Stone," says Conor Murray of Dublin. "Come show us how *you* speak."

Scarcely a day goes by that I don't hear from someone in fear. Here's an e-mail that recently came to me from Chicago:

> I'm in a professional position with the federal government and have had many successful years of avoiding speaking before groups. I need help ASAP. My shaking hands don't look good when I'm introducing someone who's won an award. Through the years I've had many bad experiences where I begin focusing on how I sound, which creates greater anxiety. I need help. Best regards, Rick.

Rick, like many of us, requires practice to get beyond his fears. He needs a *safe place* in which to speak his truth, a place in which he will not be ridiculed, criticized, or interrupted, perhaps for the first time in his life.

He can find that place with a friend as outlined in chapter 4, or even in his own mind as he imagines a completely supportive audience. Or with a few friends in the comfort of a living room or around a kitchen table.

Others will find it useful to gather family, friends, or colleagues to form a peer support Speaking Circle (see chapter 13 for instructions), or to join one that already meets in your area.

Speaking as Life

Good speaking is about the thrill of self-discovery. It puts us in the middle of life's adventure. We express what is unique about ourselves and experience our deepest connections and commonalities with other people.

"I've learned more about myself and other people in three practice sessions of transformational speaking than I did in twenty years of studying psychology and metaphysics!" said one writer.

Practicing with a supportive group lets us do on a small scale what we all want to do in the larger world: share support and community. And in the process find more of ourselves.

We already have within us everything we need to be wonderful communicators. It's just a matter of bringing our talents, powers, and magnetism to the surface.

Chapter 2

. . . .

RECLAIMING THE INNER SPEAKER:

FINDING THE POWER WE LOST

ALONG THE WAY

◎

"My experience growing up was that I had to justify what I was thinking and feeling. It just wasn't worth it most of the time, so I clammed up."

•

"I wouldn't speak in groups because I assumed I'd be challenged. I thought people were out to get me."

•

"It was a very easy presentation to give, but I found that every time I'd give it I'd be racked with anxiety."

My friend Cathy Dana has been an aspiring speaker since childhood. She told me that whenever a professional speaker came through her small town, she would always find her way to the front row to soak up the wisdom. She gave a lot of eye contact, but most speakers weren't comfortable receiving it.

She says, "I would think, 'You're the speaker; where am I supposed to look, if not at you?' But I began to think that as a speaker myself, I wasn't supposed to relate to or make contact with individuals." Cathy is now a professional speaker who *does* make intimate eye contact with individuals in her audiences, with electric results.

But many professional speakers have mastered public speaking as a *performance* event. They may be technically proficient, well-prepared, even dynamic, and get the job done. But are they live or are they Memorex? When they pause, is it for effect, or to connect?

Most public speakers seem to relate to an audience as an impersonal mass to be informed and entertained, not as a gathering of flesh-and-blood individuals. Remember, public speaking at its best is a *relationship* event, not a performance event. The audience yearns for your true self, not a mask. They want who you are on the inside, the *Inner* Speaker, not external camouflage. They want *you,* not a lecture, not a performance. You. This is the best gift you can give and the easiest. Simply give yourself. Let go. Give.

Many a competent speaker has fashioned a wonderful performance mask. Many a non-speaker has been unable to find a mask that fits. In the continuum between these two poles, people play with masks and masklessness with erratic results. But when we drop the idea of masks altogether in favor of anxious authenticity, or vibrant vulnerability, we find ourselves all in the same boat.

Fortunately, it's a sailboat, and the weather is fine. You'll find me hoisting the sail, rejoicing in the voyage home to the Inner Speaker, your true, wonderful, authentic self. So easy to give. And what a gift! The water may be choppy for a while, and the wind may ruffle some feathers, but soon the seas will settle, the wind will be at our backs, and we will speak *with* the wind, no longer *into* it.

You may understand my friend, Ernie, when he says, "Public speaking was always an uphill battle. But now that I've put my 'speaker mask' aside, I feel like I'm coasting downhill to the finish, even as I start." Ernie's Inner Speaker, his warm, real self, is open now to the audience, and everyone loves the ride.

Why We Shut Down

. . . .

Why don't we all just step up to the front of the room, embrace the audience with our presence, receive their support, and speak in a clear, heartfelt way that changes people's lives?

Why do we have to *practice* relaxing, being ourselves, and receiving from other people?

Most of us learn to edit ourselves early in life. Children do things that are not socially acceptable, especially in public—throwing food on the wall, screaming at odd moments, interrupting, saying embarrassing things about how people look, expressing negative opinions about birthday presents from Grandma. Part of being socialized is learning not to do these things. Most parents deliver that message loud and clear.

Sometimes being real *was* okay with our parents. We were given positive attention for our endearing smiles, or for the time we spontaneously hugged Uncle Albert, or presented Grandma with a handmade eightieth-birthday card. But on the whole, being real involved a lot of negative feedback. And many of us gave up the rewards to avoid the punishment.

For forty-five years I gave up the rewards of life to avoid the punishment. But being the last person who would speak up *was* my punishment—I hadn't avoided it after all. My big ideas never came out, entrapped in a shy body.

If our parents wanted us to be perfect to prove that they were decent parents, then today we may have trouble being real in front of groups. *Being perfect and being real are almost always at odds.* If we tried to be perfect, we couldn't be very real.

It's not just punishment. Some of us were laughed at, ridiculed, ignored. In my case, I grew up identified as "fat." That was my daily albatross. I was the object of ridicule and derision at home and away, from kindergarten recess to college shower rooms. It took me more than forty-five years to find my voice and "show those bastards." It was worth every minute of it.

What is the connection between being punished for being real when we were young, and being ridiculed by our peers for being different? Both issues caused us to shut down, not to trust our real selves.

What happened to *you?*

Did you have a teacher who ridiculed you when you were vulnerable? Did your Inner Speaker, your true, real self, shrink away after this, hide?

Or was it a nasty peer? A brother, a sister, a schoolmate? Did they shrink your inner voice, your true self forever? Do you still suffer today from that time of shame, pain, and ridicule? Did you lock away your Inner Speaker, your sweet, authentic self? The one that counts, the one with all that innocent power?

What happened to you?

Kids say the darndest things and many adults think it's funny to take them literally. If we announced at age five that we were going to be a nuclear physicist—or a martyred saint—we gave everybody a good laugh. From our point of view, however, we were ridiculed for being honest and vulnerable, and we learned to be careful. We learned to edit—to keep our true selves and our true feelings under wraps. Hidden away, forever.

As children, when we let fly with a piece of our authentic selves, we were sometimes punished or ridiculed. Isn't it reasonable that today we might fear to be ourselves on public occasions?

Take a moment now and imagine an audience looking at

you. You can't think of a word to say, and you remain speech-less for ten seconds. Go ahead, take ten seconds with eyes closed to do that.

Did you see a disapproving parent or teacher, or a bully schoolmate—multiplied by five, ten, fifty—by however many people are sitting out there?

Psychologists say whenever more than two people come together, we are consciously or unconsciously involved in a family dynamic. Every time we get up in front of a room, we expose ourselves to a punishing family dynamic or school dy-namic or peer group dynamic. In *public!* No wonder we get nervous, shut down, become stiff, panic, tremble, or get a dry throat. We memorize every word we're going to say, so we can feel at least a little in control. Or we adopt masks, orator-ical postures, personas, and cavalier "styles" that make us seem impervious to criticism. All of these things protect—and disconnect—us from our audience.

We feel threatened, so we defend ourselves. We really have no desire to open up and make ourselves vulnerable to these people. If they conjure up the powerful adults whose "guid-ance," criticism, or outright abuse hurt us when we were small, or the peer group bullies whose ridicule shamed us—then we're just asking for trouble if we let ourselves relax now.

The Wounded Speaker

We were wounded when we stopped trusting ourselves, stopped being ourselves. Our parents and other adults proba-bly didn't mean to inflict those wounds. But despite their good intentions, we started to deny or hide our real selves. We even started believing that the edited, quasiperson we pretended to be was who we really were.

Professor Saul Eisen, organization development consultant, says, "Even when there is no formal evaluation when I speak, a lot of people are watching me and sometimes paying a lot of money, which evokes in me a sense that I have to produce and perform."

He points out that many of us had experiences at home and in school where people important to us behaved in ways that made their love conditional on our performance. "That's a very unhelpful dynamic that produces all kinds of psychological damage," says Saul. "So many successful managers and executives are caught up in this performance-for-approval syndrome. Their success comes at a great expense."

The expense is that we become masters at meeting other people's expectations, and never meet our own.

Letting the Sun Shine In

As we saw in the previous chapter, the path to reclaiming our Inner Speaker involves massive doses of positive attention. "All the positive attention may feel narcissistic at first," says Margaret Reardon, an emergency clinic psychotherapist, "but it shores us up and this is the healing—being able to look at ourselves objectively and see the good things as well [as the bad]. We learn to see that we really *can* relax into ourselves and be real—and that people find that both fascinating and lovable."

Most of us have learned to be real one-on-one. But it takes practice to be real in public. Our Inner Speaker is hibernating. *We sometimes need group support to awaken and reclaim it.*

Our primary mode of instruction as transformational speakers—practicing into a mirror, or one-to-one, or with a supportive group—is to practice receiving support and positive acknowledgment. As we do that again and again, we start moving beyond our fears that people will be bored, punishing, or derisive. We open up to the goodwill that is actually there for us, and to people's appreciation of who we are.

"I've realized that being in front of a supportive group is my way of healing lots of wounds, of overcoming years of not being heard in my personal life, and being criticized constantly," said a teacher. "When I know I won't be told what's 'wrong' with me, I am able to take risks and not feel uneasy."

Another way support helps us heal is by allowing us to talk about those painful early experiences and release a lot of the energy behind them. Some people are terrified the first time all the attention is on them. But when we sit (or stand) through it, we find we are being completely listened to, and seen.

It is a revelation when people really listen to us and just accept whatever we say. Said a counselor, "All my life, I'd been trying to speak up, to be heard, and people told me to pipe down. But with listening support, as my voice got quieter and quieter, it commanded more and more attention!"

When people give us complete positive attention, we can let ourselves feel the old fears and know that nobody will criticize, interrupt, or psychoanalyze us. No one will take over the conversation or quip, "Cat got your tongue?" No one will imply that there's something wrong with anyone, try to fix anyone, or put anyone on the spot. We are honored for whatever we say, or don't say. It's our time and our space in which to be completely appreciated. *That* is the healing.

Sooner or later, usually sooner, the fears and defenses lift away naturally. It's not that we never feel wounded or fearful again. But we have now gained the upper hand over those experiences, and they don't stop us.

Wounded in Public, Healed in Public
. . . .

Therapist Hal Perry had been speaking in public for years, but always at the cost of enormous anxiety and energy. He was so overprepared he would have every word of the talk written out in order to recite it if necessary. He realized that it all stemmed from an incident that happened when he was twenty and going away to college. His church gave him a party, where the pastor said complimentary things about him and then asked Hal to come up and say a few words.

Overcome with emotion, Hal burst into tears and couldn't stop crying. He says, "It was a devastating experience. I'd never seen a grown man cry in public. And now *I* was doing it. From that moment on, public speaking was an agonizing experience—even when I knew the material well and wanted to share it."

In a safe, supportive setting, he mustered the courage to share his bad experience and, as a result, reversed the effects of the early incident that had caused him so much anxiety over the years. Hal says, "Being able to tell the truth about my vulnerability—and getting that rapt attention, caring, love, and acceptance started to melt the energy around that incident, minimizing the power it had over me."

When Hal gave his next professional talk a few months later, he wasn't even nervous the day before. "I had always been so wrapped up in my own anxiety that I hardly paid any attention to the audience," he says. "Now I actually *enjoy* speaking. And I can relax and relate more easily to the people in the audience."

Most of us have one or more incidents that form the basis of our discomfort at speaking in public. A safe place to tell those stories gives us an opportunity to heal.

The Magic of Being Fully Seen and Heard
. . . .

Sometimes healing happens the first time someone shares and receives support; sometimes it takes longer. But eventually, the wound is bound to heal in a loving, positive, supportive environment.

After this healing has occurred, nothing is ever the same. We have reclaimed a part of ourselves that we didn't have before. Our Inner Speaker is out! We are whole in public, so we can share ourselves with others without fear.

"I'm glad transformational speaking is being introduced in the schools," says one teacher. "We aren't accustomed to being listened to in our society, and we feel invisible a lot of the time. We run around trying to get attention—sometimes in ways that aren't very productive. When we feel fully heard, we can drop all those bells and whistles. If kids realized earlier that they aren't invisible, we'd have a better chance of educating them. It's very simple work, but it's very important and deep."

Every child has in Inner Speaker aching to be heard.

"Imagine if you had this kind of support at a family dinner table," said a legal secretary, "if everybody got even *two minutes* of attention and support to be whoever they were, and say whatever they wanted. Imagine children raised with that amount of respect."

Growing in the Greenhouse
. . . .

Professional artist George Allen Durkee sees transformational speaking practice as a greenhouse where we experience special, favorable conditions for healing and growth. He points out that if you take even the sickest plant and put it in a greenhouse with perfect conditions it will start to flourish. It will straighten up and start to produce new shoots.

Our Inner Speaker awaits, ever ready to spring forth, free.

George sees the practice of speaking into supportive listening as an opportunity to come in out of the cold and darkness we may experience at work or at home, nourish ourselves in ideal conditions, and free the Inner Speaker. "As we begin to heal and grow new shoots," he says, "we discover we have the potential to produce beautiful flowers. When it's safe to stretch, we find out what we can do."

If you can do anything you want in front of a person or a group—be outrageous, be depressed, be silent, or even rebellious—and still get those perfect, supportive conditions, you not only heal, you begin to see what you really want to say and do. You get in touch with your real voice, your Inner Speaker, and what you really have to say to people. When we have unlimited options, we go naturally to the ones that have the most resonance for us, and that's another level of healing.

When plants have had some time in the greenhouse to heal and grow, they can be transplanted back in the world and be strong. In the same way, we take our learning and healing from our support group back out into our lives. We're stronger, we know ourselves better, we're more real, and we can allow more support into our lives.

As George concludes, "The air inside this special greenhouse is made of equal parts safety and support, relaxing and receiving."

The Environment of the Mirror

Would you like to know right now whether self-consciousness is blocking you from accessing your Inner Speaker? From being your most powerful self in the world? *Sit or stand in front of a mirror.* Your challenge is to commune with yourself for three minutes. Speak or remain silent, but maintain the connection.

The extent of your self-consciousness in this situation is a measure of your performance anxiety in the world—the extent to which you block yourself from listening (and seeing) with no agenda, no judgments.

If you commune with yourself like this for five minutes a day, you will learn to listen to yourself—because you won't be able to tolerate this exercise without solving the challenge of how to be comfortable with yourself. And then you can easily transfer this comfort with yourself to groups—by seeing yourself in their eyes, in the best light. *It will end your fear of public speaking forever.*

What the Mirror Tells Us

If we can have our listener or listeners act as a mirror, reflecting back the beautiful parts of ourselves so that we can see them, often for the first time, the wound is healed—the wound inflicted when we didn't have those wonderful parts of ourselves reflected back to us as children.

When people are in the center of this "soft attention," they often come to a sudden understanding of what is important in their lives. Sometimes they have never voiced these deeper values before. In the words of one psychotherapist:

> The first time I really let in that safety and support, I heard myself say, "I want to speak more openly about the spirituality in my work. I've been disguising it on purpose so as not to offend anyone. I want to speak with

the enthusiasm and joy for spirituality that I have." That changed my work completely. Now I do speak about spirituality in my work, and it has transformed the energy level where all movement begins.

Witnessing One Another: Healing Through Shared Vulnerability

As one person becomes vulnerable in front of another, or in front of a roomful of others, and stretches to take in the support—it gets easier for *everyone* to open up. The room gets safer and safer. We see other people let go after years of holding back, and we know that our support is helping to make that possible.

One therapist pointed out, "A lot of the shame we experience as children is not just about a parent saying, 'Bad boy!' It's about them saying something like that *in front of other people*. One reason this is such healing work is that now we're not only getting positive feedback for being ourselves, but that positive feedback is also being witnessed by other people. Somehow we need that public aspect of healing to undo the earlier shame."

The Inner Speaker Awaits

Before we go deeper into the magic of reclaiming our Inner Speaker, it would be helpful to review the landscape. All of us, experienced public speakers and non-speakers alike, suffer by being disconnected from our Inner Speaker. Sufferers range from:

• Those of us with the worst stage fright who, since a bad experience around the dinner table or at school, have *never* been able to stand in front of a group—or have attempted to do so with no wits about us at all

To:

• The successful professional speaker who is hyperprepared and technique-bound to the point of bypassing a wealth of available inner resources.

Those who have come to work with me on their specific speaking challenges were brought to their knees by the unhappy consequences of being disconnected from their Inner Speaker. Their symptoms ranged from extreme stage fright to a subtle sense of alienation in the face of apparent success. The quotes on the chapter title pages run the gamut of stage fright symptoms that are relieved by reconnecting with the Inner Speaker.

Loosening the "Muscle"

Time and again over the past ten years I have witnessed every one of these symptoms and a host of others abate and disappear in my classes, sometimes instantly, when the Inner Speaker is accessed.

I have seen and heard it so many times I can describe the typical moment of "magic." It's as if a tightened muscle, centered in the speaker's mind, throat, or heart, suddenly relaxes. When this "muscle," which has kept the Inner Speaker separated and shut off, suddenly loosens, a fountain of easy expressiveness begins to flow.

Because this muscle, as I am calling it, is so habitually tight, the person has no idea it exists—or that an intact Inner Speaker awaits just on the other side of a thin veil of fears. For many of us, the muscle was first contracted in childhood by a survival instinct that told us our life depended on our *not telling our whole truth.*

It was further tensed in youth when we internalized the negative messages we were given about our ability to speak. And the muscle was tightened to the point of strangulation in adulthood by years of practice.

This tight muscle acts like a valve that's stuck in the off position and disconnects our wheel-spinning Outer Speaker from our infinitely resourceful Inner Speaker.

The Rewards of Reconnecting

When the Inner Speaker finally emerges, we can take delight in the fact that it has matured along with the rest of us, like a fine wine. We just forgot it was stored down there in the basement!

Once you loosen the muscle that has kept it mute, the Inner Speaker will find its way out, if that's what you sincerely want, and be delighted to run the show. Here are the benefits of continuing to let it develop and have its say:

• *On informal occasions.* You will be able to stand up at the drop of a hat in front of any size group, anytime, anywhere, and trust yourself to express what the occasion calls for!

• *On formal occasions.* With much less preparation than ever before, you will be able to access what you already know—precisely when you need it, intuitively.

Different and the Same
. . . .

One of the most healing things we can experience is our common humanity with other people. When Inner Speakers are reclaimed, they reveal that we are all absolutely unique, and also that we are very much alike.

"Witnessing other people speaking their truths, I experience diversity on a whole other level," says a computer consultant. "It would be impossible for me to imitate anyone out there."

Another speaker sees this work as "a real isolation-breaker, a way of tuning in to how similar we are. It's a community builder because you get unconditional support and that bonds you. Everyone is vulnerable and has to trust, so you relate to people in a fresh and spontaneous way."

We reclaim our Inner Speaker in order to become the person we were meant to be. To let go of the masks and defenses we adopted to spare ourselves pain. To be the person we really are—not the person others wanted us to be. We heal so that we can be real. And that is the subject of the next chapter.

Chapter 3

. . . .

BEING YOURSELF:

THE KEY TO COMPELLING

RAPT ATTENTION

The most compelling thing we can do— in life, *and* in front of the room—is be authentic.

It is the simplest thing in the world.

But rare in public speaking. It doesn't always happen even in individual communication. "I'm real with my family and close friends," we may think. But even with these people we often get trapped in roles, habits, and expectations that hide our real selves.

> "I always feel I'm letting myself down by speaking from a controlled place, that it doesn't meet what a deeper part of me wants to express."
>
> •
>
> "I am a successful speaker who just isn't able to be myself in public."
>
> •
>
> "I look at the audience as the enemy."

True power lies in authenticity—tapping into our own values and experiences, making sure that what we say is what we believe. Authentic, honest, real speaking offers us a way to find and express deeper, truer parts of ourselves—both with strangers in an audience and with the people we love most.

"Just Be Here"

. . . .

The deepest, truest part of ourselves shows up—in its purest form—in our very presence. David Roche tells this defining story about presence:

I had been traveling from San Francisco to Los Angeles to help care for my friend in the last months of his life. I would ask him, "What do you need? What should I do? I know! I'll make some Jell-O. We have lime or black cherry."

And he would say, "Just be here."

I'd say, "There's Cool Whip!"

He'd say, "Just be here."

I thought he was not in touch with his needs, or was too shy to say what he really wanted. Perhaps he had dementia. But after a while I caught on that what he wanted was my full presence. We would sit on the couch for hours, saying nothing, his head on my lap, listening to the Mass in B Minor. He wasn't talking much by then anyway.

One thing he did say often, and sometimes, I thought, inappropriately, was—"Good for you. Good for you."

One Sunday night I was getting ready to fly back to San Francisco and he asked me to stay through the week. I hesitated. I was afraid to call my job and tell them I wasn't showing up. Then I was flooded with the knowledge that I did want to "just be there." That was a moment of grace for me. I didn't make a choice. It was given to me—a moment of absolute clarity when love took priority.

I said yes, and he said, "Good for you." That was the last week of his life. And that moment of grace changed my life as well. Allowed me to listen to my inner voice. Gave me the gift of presence, authenticity. Gave me clarity, resolved my own personal fears, doubts. Allowed me to return to San Francisco and propose to my darling Marlena. The gift of presence from my dying friend.

What Is "Real"?

Being real means just being here. Standing before people in an open, vulnerable way without roles or masks or expectations of any kind. We connect with people just as we are right now. And receive their support. Our priority is to be completely present with them, and to let whatever we say come out of that relationship.

I have seen people stand in front of a room reading a dictionary—and keep people enthralled. How? By being here, now, present.

Jana Stanfield, professional speaker and million-record-selling Nashville songwriter, asks, "You know what means the most to me of what we've learned here? Total freedom to be exactly who I am.

"No pretenses, no smoke, no mirrors. What a revelation to find that my real, human self is what audiences like best. Even my *business* audiences. I think it's because it frees *them* to be their own most real, human selves."

Authenticity comes not so much from what we say, but how we say it. Not from telling the truth or revealing our deepest, darkest secrets. Being real is more than that.

Our Presence Says More Than Our Words

Who we are speaks more loudly than what we say—with business associates, in personal relationships, and in front of the room.

What we tell people may be extremely valuable, but how they *feel* in relation to us determines whether or not they hear us, trust us, and act on what we say. If we are real with them, they will pay attention. They will believe what we say, and be inspired to do something in response. If we aren't completely present—or if we're wearing any kind of mask—they can easily dismiss or resent us.

Remember when you took an instant dislike to a speaker or teacher? And resisted what he or she said—even though it made good sense and was of possible benefit? We *know* when a speaker is cranking out a prepackaged message but isn't really passionate about the subject. If someone is trying to sell us something to make a quota, we know it.

We may not understand why, but we know something is wrong. Something is not as it seems, and we become wary. What we're hearing is different from what we're feeling. That dissonance makes us edgy. We want to put some distance between ourselves and the speaker, both mentally and physically. We certainly won't buy what he or she is selling.

According to San Francisco marketing consultant Jamie Silver, "What really sells people on anything is the authenticity of the individual. You have to tell them about the product or service, but they have to believe you and trust you. And when you're authentic, they do trust you. They can't help but want to connect with you when you connect with them on that level."

Bonnie, a wife and mother, put it another way: "People are

not as motivated by what goes on in the head as they are by what goes on in the heart."

Our message is important—but the depth of our commitment to that message and our relationship with the audience are even more important.

It's Not the Crime; It's the Cover-Up

Richard Nixon learned this lesson during the Watergate investigations, and it also holds true for public speaking.

What makes people uneasy is not that the speaker is nervous or fearful; it's that the speaker is upset about being nervous or afraid, and trying to cover it up or make it go away. If we acknowledge our nervousness, our audience is fine. But they cringe if we pretend to be cavalier, arrogant, nonchalant, or blasé—and they can *feel* our unease. They know we're lying. And they'll have trouble believing anything else we say.

"When I got comfortable with my shyness, I didn't mind talking to groups," says the head of a decorating firm. "Situations that used to terrify me—like talking to a board—became pretty simple. I used to agonize and pretend to be so confident. But now I'm just myself and it works better. *Much* better."

We can be anxious, but at the same time completely connected with the group and compelling their rapt attention. We feel the anxiety, but we don't judge or hide it. We may even talk about it, and about *why* we're nervous.

Being just the way we are—even when that isn't how we think we *should* be—is being real.

The "Real Zone"
. . . .

We all know how it feels when the person in front of the room is truly open, relaxed, and authentic, reaching out to accept our support and relate to us.

The air becomes electric. Right? At the same time, an enormous feeling of relief settles over the room. Everyone breathes more easily. Every pair of eyes is riveted on the speaker. That person is sharing something very personal. It might be about love, or pain, or growing, or just about being more productive at work, but it touches something deep within us. It resonates with what we know about life, and gives us a shared sense of what it is to be human. Our external activities and experiences may be very different from the speaker, but we know the speaker understands something about us.

"When I hit the 'real zone,' I know it," says Judith Parker, who owns a speaker's agency. "All of a sudden, I connect with myself and the audience. It's like playing tennis, and hitting the ball exactly right on the racquet, in the sweet spot. There's no energy spent; it just flows and I feel that connection. After the first time I had that experience in front of a supportive group, I could re-create it consistently in front of groups of fifty or even hundreds."

The "real zone" isn't a place where we arrive once and then stay without having to think about it again. Our authenticity is different in every moment because every moment is different. We need to renew our connection with other people in every moment—just as actors in a play must speak the same lines every night, but also make each new night fresh for each new audience.

Why Being Real Is Mesmerizing
. . . .

People pay rapt attention to us when we are deeply, openly ourselves. And when we learn to do that in front of a room? We become a tremendous force for good.

"We don't always bring our real self forward," says a personnel manager. "We bring our capacities, but not our vulnerabilities. It's a challenge to be present in that way out there in the world. But people's response is overwhelmingly positive—when we are."

If we are real, people tend to enjoy us. An artist told me that she used to feel judged by what she saw as "the patriarchy"—business people, conservatives, successful career people. "I blamed them for not accepting me as I am," she says. "But since I dropped the defensiveness and just present myself and my truth, they come into my heart! I now feel equal to those people who used to intimidate me. And that is wonderful."

The more we open up and receive people's support, the more of ourselves we discover. And the more we share with *them,* the more they receive *us* and our message. It's a fabulous, inspirational, upward cycle.

"I'm *open* to groups now," says a biologist. "I know now that people really do want to get to know me. When I come into groups knowing that, it becomes a reality. When I came into groups thinking the opposite, they really *didn't* want to get to know me."

When we are genuinely ourselves, we give our listeners permission to be genuinely *themselves.* Being real is irresistible. If we are relaxed enough to stand in all of our greatness and vulnerability—then our listeners feel comfortable with *their* greatness and vulnerability. It's like a mirror. Being real in front of a group holds up a mirror to the audience. Lets everyone enjoy the richness of the human spirit in one another. Not a common experience in our society, right? People can't get enough of it.

"You have to perform when you're in front of an audience. That's what we were all taught," says John Sullivan, business consultant. "You have to be what people want. An image. But what I've learned through authentic speaking is the opposite. Now I let who I really am come out and interact with who other people really are. The reason it's so powerful is—people are looking everywhere for exactly that kind of connection in this world."

John Harrison, a writer and former stutterer who coaches members of the stuttering community in public speaking, told me: "Stutterers grow up self-conscious and are usually very uncomfortable in front of a group. Audience members immediately sense this. And because they pick up on the speaker's feelings, they become uncomfortable themselves."

John points out that film directors play upon the audience's quickness to react to what others are feeling. For example, when someone pulls a gun on the hero, the director generally cuts to a reaction shot. Is the hero reacting fearfully? Then the audience will worry. On the other hand, if the hero is acting nonchalant, then the audience figures that the situation is under control, and they relax.

John teaches stutterers that they don't have to be fluent or perfect, don't have to put up a facade: "Just show up as who you are," he tells them. "Show up as real. If you're having trouble speaking, be up front about it. If you're feeling scared, allow the fear to be there, perhaps even acknowledge it." (See Appendix C for more information on how this method can help alleviate stuttering problems.)

When your audience realizes that you're being honest

about how you feel—and that you're willing to reveal your real self—they're much more likely to settle back and connect with you and what you have to say. When people put their real selves forward, they often are mesmerizing. Their words may not flow smoothly right away—but they are mesmerizing.

A smooth flow of words and ideas is usually an outgrowth, though not the emphasis, of this way of honesty. The emphasis is on being real, becoming comfortable with ourselves—which causes our listeners to lean back and just luxuriate in this rare permission to be comfortable with themselves.

Your Real Voice

People sometimes ask me for voice coaching. How can they master mellifluous tones? How can they lose an accent? How can they cover up a speech problem? The first thing I do is give them this quote by Elbert Hubbard, a nineteenth-century philosopher:

> The best way to cultivate the voice is not to think about it.
>
> Actions become regal only when they are unconscious; and the voice that convinces, that holds us captive, that leads and lures us on, is used by its owner unconsciously.
>
> Fix your mind on the thought, and the voice will follow.
>
> If the voice is allowed to come naturally, easily and gently, it will take on every tint and emotion of the mind.
>
> The way to cultivate the voice is not to cultivate it.

Image consultant Jordan Hart always imagined that there was one way to speak, with standard techniques and gestures, a way to breathe and use one's voice. If you practiced long enough you'd become an effective speaker. Suffering awful stage fright compounded by a "nasal" voice, she finally sought help from a professional speech coach.

"She told me that my voice was arrested at an adolescent level," says Jordan. The coach would be able to fix it with breathing exercises if Jordan came to her every week for a while.

Not up for that, she gave up on public speaking.

When she finally got support for her *real* voice, she uncovered an effective style that works beautifully with her natural way of speaking. "Suddenly public speaking is no longer outside of me," she says.

What Being Real Is Not

Being real should be as natural as the sun rising and the grass growing, right? But often, unfortunately, the training we receive as speakers actually *keeps* us from being authentic—acts as camouflage for our real selves, hides who we really are.

This professional training usually includes such performance techniques as stylized gestures, carefully planned movements onstage, a practiced vocal tone for every sentence, strategically placed "meaningful" pauses, and knowing exactly when we will slow down or speed up our speech. All these techniques are attempts to create substance and meaning through *style*—and it just can't be done that way.

Bebe Borowitz, manager of a sales team at a high-tech company, was asked by her boss a number of times to conduct seminars around the country. She always declined in terror.

"Finally," she says, "they sent me to the top-of-the-line corporate presentation training program where I learned the techniques for structuring and delivering a good canned presentation. But I still had the terror underneath."

In desperation, Bebe faced her fear dead on, speaking about it to a supportive group. "With that as a starting point," she says, "I was quickly amazed by my ability to look into the eyes of an audience and speak authentically from my essence to them. From that I went directly to doing those sales seminars—and enjoying them."

Many speaking programs give lip service to speaking authentically. But what they actually teach is *mechanics.*

It's as if they were using a book of techniques for forming a relationship—one that recommended specific words and behaviors to produce certain results. On the first date, for instance, your instructions might be to go to a Chinese restaurant and a movie. When you proposed, the stage direction might be to kneel down on your right knee and pause for three seconds before speaking.

That's not how real relationships work, and it's not how effective speaking works, either.

In fact, people who start out with coaching that makes them look "polished" from day one often miss the chance to let their own natural style emerge. They get everything all planned out and practiced—instead of seeing what kinds of gestures, movements, and vocal tone evolve organically out of their own enthusiasm and personality, and the content of their message.

When we've used these performance techniques for a long time and they have brought us some success, we may feel too vulnerable to let go of them.

Janis was a skilled public speaker. She knew how to stand

up and entertain and was very comfortable doing it the traditional way. Transformational speaking was a new and profound experience for her because she had to go through the process of stripping away a facade.

"When I began to show up as a more real and authentic speaker," she says, "it impacted every area of my life and all my relationships. I was more present, more genuine, and more vulnerable. I let people see me more, so I got more love, more trust. More everything!"

A magazine once asked if I could provide any tips for an article on "stage skills."

"Yes," I said. "Realize that stage skills are overrated. The best thing we can do is to open our hearts, and slow down enough to enjoy ourselves and be with the individuals in our audience. From this thriving relationship, stage skills and a unique style will evolve quickly and naturally on their own."

The difference between technical instruction and instruction in being ourselves, real and honest, is the difference between being instructed to "pause for five beats" and being told to stay silent with our audiences and let our words sink in, as we gaze at individual persons in the audience and "listen" to them get it.

We want to stand together with our audience, not above them, to speak from the inside out, rather than from the outside in. Our insides speak to their insides—instead of our outsides speaking to their outsides. Intimacy, not distance.

There's a huge difference between *performing* for someone and *relating* to someone. "I know a lot about relationships and very little about performing," said one psychologist. "This shift brought to life all the work I've done in my personal therapy and as a therapist. And gave me a way to carry it over authentically to a speaking situation. It's so much better for me this way. I don't have to have an anxiety headache, nor do I have to obsess about it ahead of time."

My goal is to change public speaking from a performance event to a relationship event. "I never want to get caught up in the slickness," says another professional speaker. "We have to forget about being good, and remember to be *ourselves.*"

Finding Our Natural Style

We can't go wrong when we're ourselves, because nobody does "us" as well as we do.

Authentic speaking encourages us to find our own individual style. That may take a little time and involve some discomfort because we don't get to wear masks, but the result is a way of being with audiences that is natural, organic, and effortless. And it achieves astounding results.

Sometimes people actually have their natural styles coached *out* of them. For instance, a coach might tell someone, "Don't speak so fast! Slow down!" But if this person is a Type A personality or from New York, his natural style may *be* fast! He may talk fast, walk fast, think fast, and look and feel strange if he is forced to be any other way. Slowing down could actually take away his power.

He might find it helpful to pause frequently so that Type B's and non–New Yorkers can catch up—and so that he himself can breathe, recapture the connection, and make sure he's still heading in the direction he wants to go in. But talking fast can be very effective for him if that's his natural style.

"Finding my own voice is about being free," says one real estate developer. "When I'm up there in my truth, not doing it any particular way, just being myself, I see people sort of wake up, like they understand. I'm not speaking anyone else's speech, not doing anyone else's thing. I'm just being me, being present—coming from my heart."

Modeling Our Topic

Another way to be real in front of the room is to *live* our message, to become the embodiment and model of our topic.

Elma Garcia, director of TV commercials, had an unexpected opportunity to model her topic. She had just flown into town expecting to make a presentation for five people in a little conference room. She was told at the last minute that she'd be doing it for four hundred potential clients in the auditorium.

"My knees went weak," she remembers, "but I just decided to be me and let the chips fall where they might. I hung out with them, told stories, talked about work, and wove everything together as I would with a friend."

Her subject happened to be the power of truth and keeping our integrity, and she modeled that by being herself with them, and keeping her own truth and integrity. "I became the speech," she says, "and embodied what I said. People came up afterward and said, 'I didn't know it was going to be that inspirational'—and it came just from relaxing and being myself."

Being Real Is Good Business

Being real isn't just a New Age concept. Or some therapist's good idea. It's the wave that business leaders are riding—not only because it is good for our health and well-being, but because it produces results.

Larry Prochazka, a Colorado trainer for Fortune 500 companies, offers this advice:

Presence—realness—authenticity: *these* are the qualities which evoke an audience to be authentic.

It is not the trainers' experience, not their training, and not their background that determines who is effective—and even who is hired. It is their ability to be human and relate as people to the individuals in the room.

A formal presenter invites an audience to relate formally, which prevents people from diving into the real issues underlying current problems. A "cute" presenter who uses clever stories and jokes invites resentment and makes people ask, "Why don't they *relate* to me? Why don't they get *real?*"

Safety is essential for deep work to take place. A real, authentic, human being who embraces and receives an audience creates a safe environment in which to share and discuss. Deeper issues, honest issues—identified at a personal level—result in change.

So many different waves of training have swept through the corporate world in the past ten years, many with little impact. Companies are starting to realize that training doesn't make as much difference as the *trainer* does.

People can read trainers. They can tell who they are, what they stand for, what their character is, whether they trust them to work with their people. Develop more of the human being, bring more to the table, and watch training effectiveness *improve* dramatically.

How Do We Get to "Real"?

We can't "try" to be real. We can just relax and let ourselves be whoever we are—calm, hopeful, nervous, shut down, ecstatic, sad, focused, joyful, quiet, angry, or blissful.

When we relax, remember that we already *are* ourselves, and we settle down into genuine, supportive connections with other people—everything starts to come together. We can almost *feel* ourselves entering the "real zone."

A dyad (two people) or a peer support Speaking Circle with as few as three people is a wonderful place to practice doing this. It seems simplistic to say that having unconditional support allows us to go within and be real, but I've been watching it happen since 1989, and it works every time!

We all need other people to reflect back to us who we are. We needed that as children, and we need it as adults. It's in our connection with others that we find our real selves and experience ourselves in a new and fuller way through their eyes.

"My goal is to come from my soul, so that I can reach the souls of the people in the audience," says one aspiring professional speaker. "When I am being myself, whoever that is, people are touched. Then I can share my truth and my inner work with them, and they *get* it."

Once we find where "real" is, we can start living, and communicating, from that place more and more, in front of the room—and in life.

To get to "real," we also need permission to experiment. Sometimes we have to act out all the "unreal" parts of ourselves, the personas and masks, before we can connect with our truest selves. We need a place to blow off steam and make "mistakes" in the company of loving, supportive people. We get all the surface cover-ups out of the way, and our radiant, unadulterated selves emerge.

The Basic Reconnect Exercise

The basic exercise to enter into this work takes five minutes and may be done with a partner who has read and understood this book up to this point, and is sincerely committed to a five-minute test run. Or you can try this exercise alone, playing both parts.

If you are willing to suspend any disbelief for five minutes and follow these guidelines to the letter, this exercise will open your eyes to a wonderful world of speaking ease and prepare you for the rest of this book. If it doesn't provide you with an immediate Inner Speaker experience, it will at least make you want to take another five-minute stab at it.

Sit in a quiet room facing each other at a comfortable conversational distance. (If you are doing this alone, sit facing an empty chair.) Use chairs with relatively straight backs. Set a timer, one that doesn't tick loudly, for two minutes. Or use a clock or watch you can glance at easily without getting distracted.

One person is the listener and timer, and the other is the "speaker." That word is in quotes because the "speaker" doesn't have to speak. The listener does most of the work. (If you are doing this solo, you might imagine the world's greatest listener sitting across from you.)

Instructions to listener: Aside from keeping track of the time, keep soft, supportive, receptive eyes on the speaker for the full two minutes (except for glances at the time, if you're using a clock). This *soft listening* is the key to the entire experience. The eyes are not staring. You do not nod encouragingly or smile a lot. You are open, pleasant, still, available. You see the highest good in the speaker and expect nothing. You let any judgments pass.

This may not be easy work, but it is wonderful practice because it is exactly the kind of listening that pays huge dividends in life. The speaker, on the other hand, has "less than no work" to do.

Instructions to speaker: The listener says softly, "Okay, you're on" and starts the timing. Don't speak for at least one deep breath, and for the time it takes to fully notice and appreciate the listening. You may stay silent for the whole two minutes. Avoid making off-hand comments out of nervousness. Rather, feel the nervousness. *Feel whatever you feel. Think whatever you think.* But stay softly available to the soft eyes listening across from you. Speak into them only if you are moved to speak. Stop to breathe. Stop to remember that all you are doing is being the center of attention while someone supports you in doing so. *You have nothing to do.* With two minutes to bask in the attentive, available support, any attempt to *do* anything gets in the way. When there is a sense of any effort, or pressure to do something, remember that the only guideline is to put a priority on receiving the listening and support for being *exactly who you are.*

The listener signals with a gently raised finger at the two-minute mark (or the timer goes off). The speaker finishes in roughly fifteen seconds, and acknowledges being done. The listener takes a deep breath and says, "Thank you."

Switch roles with no conversation about what just happened. (If you are doing this alone, switch seats.) The new speaker takes a breath, and the cycle continues.

That's it!

What happened? Talk about how this experience felt, rather than about the content that may have come up.

Can you sense that systematically repeating this exercise is the next step down the road to full reconnection with your

Inner Speaker? That it is an extremely valuable tool for both your public speaking and your private listening?

If you do, and you are willing to stay with it through periods of "stuckness," even if it means finding a new partner, you cannot fail.

"I was doing this exercise regularly with my husband, Al, when he got transferred," Judy told me. "It would be two months before I could join him in the new city. There was no one else I wanted to partner with in the small town, and I found myself on the phone with him, bemoaning the situation." They hit on the idea of continuing the exercise over the phone, each looking at a photograph of the other. It worked!

Letting Ourselves Be
. . . .

We enrich our experience in many different ways when we allow ourselves to be real. Here are a few of the benefits that transformational speakers realize:

- *Relaxation* "Whether I'm talking with friends, associates, or people I've just met, I am more real. I say what I really want to say, without being worried about how I am coming across or whether I am getting emotional. Most of the time I am able to take my time and breathe, and let the words form naturally."
- *Articulation* "I have discovered a new ability to be with strangers—to speak up in situations where I used to sit on my hands. And on my tongue. My life has improved a great deal since I have been able to say what I'm thinking without feeling I will be destroyed by others."
- *Expressiveness* "I used to be very reserved. I'd listen and bring others out, but when it came to me, it's as if I

had a computer in my head calculating my role with each person—how much I could expose before they'd hold something against me. Now I take delight in being who I am and telling people about it. I enjoy entertaining and expressing my humorous side."

• *Authenticity* "I've learned to accept my own idiosyncrasies as a speaker. And as a human being. Rather than learning a formula that fits a different personality type and mind-set. I can relax and have fun, and let my natural enthusiasm come through rather than using artificial hype."

• *Flexibility* "I love being able to express different emotions—vulnerability, sadness, whatever. My whole childhood, I never cried in front of anyone. I would leave rather than cry, and now I've cried in front of numerous groups because that's what came up. And I know it's a valuable—even a generous—thing to do, to share your whole self in that way."

• *Power* "I know that my biggest selling point is me. And I can feel the difference between trying to be someone else and being who I really am and just trusting that."

Living Onstage

The greatest joy in speaking comes when there is no difference between how we live onstage and how we live offstage.

Singer/songwriter Carly Simon once told an interviewer on *Good Morning America* that she had terrible stage fright and could never hide it because everything she was feeling showed on her face. If she was angry, frustrated, or frightened, everybody knew it. She told the interviewer that this wasn't always "appropriate."

But as she was being interviewed, Carly was extraordinarily radiant and lovely. She wasn't just giving an interview, she was living life fully, as *herself.* And when she sang, she wasn't just singing—she was living. There seemed to be no difference between how she was onstage and how she was off-stage.

Marilyn King, a two-time Olympic pentathlete who speaks to corporate audiences on "Olympian Thinking," says that her biggest challenge was to believe that she could just step onto the stage, connect with people, and trust that the right words would come. Some years ago, she had a chance to try it out.

Just prior to her keynote address at the annual New York State Wellness Conference, she went back to her room on the other side of the college campus to study the opening and closing of her talk. Dissatisfied with the closing, she threw it in the garbage. After reworking it, she tossed the second version. After discarding the third version, she said to herself: "The hell with it, I'll do the whole talk the way I learned it in that 'be authentic' speaking class. I'll just be present."

So Marilyn left all the notes in her room and walked across the campus. "Halfway across I stopped in my tracks, stunned at what I'd decided to do, but there was no time to go back," she remembers.

At the venue there was a huge stage with three rows of black curtains. Standing in the dark, behind the third black curtain, astonished at what she had decided to do, she flashed on a recurring fantasy of bringing a stool out and sitting at the edge of the stage. And as she stood there stunned, she heard, "And here's Marilyn King!" Taking a step forward, she stumbled over something. It was a tall, four-legged stool! She took it out with her and ceremoniously put it at the front of the stage.

She found herself saying, "I've always wanted to do this," and the crowd burst into applause. To this day, Marilyn doesn't know why. "During that talk," she fondly recollects, "every time a voice came up in my head, whatever aside came to my mind, I gave voice to it. I had a blast!"

Marilyn always wanted to add more levity to her talks but had not been very successful in her attempts at it. To her astonishment, "When I watched the videotape of this one, I counted forty-two bursts of laughter. I got a standing ovation and was booked for five wellness conferences out of that appearance!"

Transformational speaking is about bringing our lives to the stage, and taking what we get on the stage to the rest of our lives. The best and easiest way to do that is to be the people we really are, both onstage and in our lives.

Chapter 4

. . . .

LISTENING WITH THE HEART:

LETTING OTHERS "BE HEARD NOW!"

◉

Transformational listening: Listening in a way that opens up the possibility of essential change in both the listener and the speaker.

On May 27, 1994, I spent five minutes with my mom, the night before she died. She wasn't communicating, so all I could do was listen to her silence. In that five minutes, I fully heard her for the first time in my life.

My mother was a great listener. She taught me how to listen lovingly to people's silences, as well as to their words. As a speaking coach, I've learned that the key to being fully heard is to listen to your audience *even while you are speaking to them.* It's a secret that gives you tremendous power in a world where people often seem too busy or too apathetic to pay attention.

> "I am so polished that people can't see my fear. I excel publicly, but feel like a failure privately."
>
> •
>
> "I have always felt disconnected from groups."
>
> •
>
> "The only thing I can hear when I'm up there is my heart pounding through my shirt pocket."

Listening in a way that opens up the possibility of essential change in both the listener and the speaker may be called "transformational listening." It is at the heart of effective speaking. It is also the key ingredient in successful relationships, business skills such as management and team building, and all good communication.

Author/journalist Gregg Levoy believes that "Listening is incredibly underrated. Most people are serial talkers. It tests your most concerted social skills to be nice, and to extricate yourself at the same time." Gregg says, "We all need a place to be heard. Something formal, with regularity, and with others not sitting there squirming and resentful, waiting for their turn."

What We Crave

What do we all crave more than anything else? To be fully seen and fully heard—and to be accepted exactly the way we are. If we are the ones who are doing the listening and accepting, then we have what the world wants most!

There is a humorous line among professional speakers that sincerity is the key to this business, and when you can fake *that,* you've got it made. Some take this notion seriously, believing that seasoning a canned talk with a few earnest remarks will win the day. But more and more, audiences feel the disrespect.

We who care, who are "heart speakers," authentic speakers, know that people deserve our respect. We recognize that each moment is fluid, each person unique. And that we have to keep listening all the time for people's reactions and energy flow.

We accept our audience exactly the way they are, without

trying to fix them, change them, or make them better—and without dwelling on how they "should" be. They may be tired, cranky, excited, or hostile, or warm and friendly. They may shift from one of these moods to another midway through our talk, or every five minutes. They may be eating their lunches. Or talking to one another. We let them do whatever they do.

People who feel heard and accepted listen to other people. The more we listen to and accept our audience, the more they will hear us. When we give people what everybody wants more than anything else on earth, speaking feels like gliding on the wind rather than trudging up a hill.

The Art of Listening

We're told that enlightened people see with the third eye. Their vision goes beyond the physical plane to an intuitive level where they perceive a deeper truth. In speaking from the heart, we learn to listen with the third ear. We hear in a different dimension—beyond the words to what people are actually sensing and feeling, and even to who they are.

Allen Klein, who calls himself a "Jollytologist," was brought in to speak at a corporation that was laying off twelve hundred people. His task was to "lighten up" the situation for the survivors. As soon as he stood up in front of them and looked at their faces, he could sense that his regular humor program would fall on deaf ears. "To go right into my material would be to ignore the reality of what was happening," he told me.

So Allen let them know that he realized how difficult their situation was. He asked them, "Can humor help here? Can it relieve the tension?" Then he thought out loud, "I think that first we need to let the anger come up." He gave individuals the opportunity to express themselves, and after fifteen minutes he sensed relief in the room, the feeling that "We can breathe again! We can go on. We will survive." Then he eased into his regular program for the rest of the hour.

As we look out into the audience, we see the extraordinary beauty of each person, and the light within each individual. The beauty we see out there is reflected in our own eyes, and that is what makes transformational speakers so irresistible. People see their own best nature mirrored in us.

This is not merely the "active listening" taught in some communications courses, with techniques like asking the right questions, mirroring body language, and paraphrasing back to the person what you are hearing. "Heart listening" is a heart connection, a new dimension of hearing that honors people and makes them feel fully heard, without any demand for them to perform or to act in any particular way.

This kind of listening takes place at the soul level. It is a fluid process that can't be codified into a list of action steps or "to do"s. It is a place we come from, rather than an action we take.

Maureen Gilmartin recently spoke about the real-estate field for career day at her local high school. The students were polite but not responsive. Maureen's authenticity had usually shown up as gentle inspiration, but as she "listened" to their response and watched their slumping posture, it was obvious she wasn't getting where she wanted to go with these youngsters. She suddenly found herself being loud and energetic, which brought them in.

"They wanted the cheerleader in me to come out and tell them 'Go for it!' So I did," she says. "They started waking up and moving to the edge of their seats." The change in style came naturally, in response to the situation, as might have occurred with her own children.

Most of us have done this kind of listening in close personal relationships. We sense where the other person is, even when no words are exchanged. We can feel their anger, love, sadness, frustration, elation, confusion, or concern. If we love them, *we let them be there.* We don't withdraw from them, even when we are put off or afraid. We stay connected, in the relationship, whether it's ecstatic or uncomfortable. We hear what they say, and we also appreciate how precious silence can be.

As speakers from the heart, we bring this same openness and sensitivity into our relationships with casual friends, business associates, customers, clients—or a room full of people. We receive the presence and support of others, whether they are sitting in an audience, having breakfast with us, hashing through a difficult business deal, or about to put us way over the top of our sales quota.

Listening with the heart can't be taught, but it can be *caught* by watching people do it and practicing it ourself.

Mortgage broker Judy Shaper says: "When we practice listening for the positive, we begin to hear everyone with a different ear." She explains that listening with a positive ear nourishes the seeds of joy within her. Then, when the seeds of negativity sprout, there is little room for them to flourish and take root.

"Listening to others with my full being helps to water the seeds of positivity," Judy says. "Afterwards I feel happier and closer to my true spirit and experience more comfort just being in the world."

Listen *While* You Are Speaking?

The key to tapping into your Inner Speaker is simple. But it involves a communication skill that is underdeveloped in our culture. Any reasonably intelligent person can learn it. When learned well it has a *huge* impact on communication and success.

I am referring to the capacity to listen while you are speaking: To listen to yourself. To listen to the persons you are speaking to. To listen to the stillness behind the noise.

To access your Inner Speaker, you need to act as if the listening you are speaking into is more important than what you have to say. Putting a priority on listening over speaking is the formula for instant rapport and true charisma.

Think of a person in your life, or from your past, who is smart and vibrant, yet very easy for almost anyone to be with. Imagine this person's face as he or she speaks to you.

I'm imagining my Uncle Max, who died thirty years ago but still lives delightfully in my memory. Even when I was a little child, Uncle Max never spoke *at* me, or even *to* me; he seemed to speak *with* me, even when he was doing all the talking. Looking back, I recognize now that he had the capacity to gently and closely listen to me even as he spoke. And everyone felt that way about Uncle Max. Can you sense that trait in the person you have selected?

It may seem that you either have this trait or you don't—that most of us don't, and there's no way to get it. I certainly didn't have it. But through a series of life's twists and turns, I discovered how to get it and how to teach it—and "it" turns out to be the key to public speaking with ease and without fear.

Listening with No Agenda

When I present workshops at business conferences, I always ask the million-dollar salespeople in fields from commercial real estate to radio advertising, "What is the key element to your success?"

It always comes down to some version of "listening with no agenda." They mean having a conversation with a client or potential client with no attempt to sell—but rather putting 100 percent effort into sincerely discovering the state of mind and needs of the person.

When I then ask how many associates in their company and in their industry follow their lead, they invariably frown and indicate "hardly any." Many of these sales leaders train others, and they tell me—with a hint of resignation and disappointment—that in their experience the capacity to listen without an agenda *cannot be taught*.

I agree. Listening with no agenda—and listening while speaking—cannot be taught. But I have discovered that in a certain environment these skills can be *caught*. My life work—my calling—*is creating such environments*.

Quality sales training does attempt to teach people to listen with no agenda—using role play and other techniques—but often fails to significantly improve the salesperson's *basic* relationships with individuals and groups.

Remember—the environment that allows you to listen with no agenda, and to listen *while* speaking, is the same environment that allows you to tap into your Inner Speaker and gain the capacity to speak with ease and eloquence to groups of any size.

I once did a talk in a glorious church sanctuary on interviewing skills for people in career transition. As I stood before the audience, awed by the setting, I found myself "listening" to the church. Before getting into my subject matter, I called the group's attention to the setting. Allowing a minute of silence, I asked them to really look around and pay attention to this place. This took their minds off their immediate problem, and made a good transition to the need to establish a strong listening presence in interviews. But I hadn't calculated this; it was merely the result of my listening to the setting with no agenda.

Mindfulness Speaking

When we stand before the audience and receive their support, the feelings of connection and love that rush through us usually stop our mental chatter. We are swept up into a serene, yet energetic state very similar to what meditators describe.

One problem some people face in transformational speaking is that when it clicks, it seems much too easy. Many of us are so resistant to giving up control we'd rather fail than sail. I like to say, with only slight exaggeration, that "it takes less than no work" to speak effortlessly. Any attempt to do anything but *be* will get in the way.

Melody Ermachild Chavis wrote *Altars in the Street* about finding compassion in the midst of chaos and violence through her work as a private investigator for the defense on death row, and as a community activist in a troubled, violent neighborhood. She says, "My spiritual practice as a Buddhist is to really be present with an audience, giving full attention to them and to what I'm doing in what might be called 'mindfulness speaking.' "

Melody's spiritual practice was put to the test when a professor at Golden Gate Law School asked her to lecture her class of third-year law students about the death penalty:

I got a very hostile question from a young man who was going to be a prosecutor. He challenged me on my anti-capital punishment position. He angrily asked me how I would feel if *my* daughter was murdered. How dare I be forgiving to these people?

I could have given him statistics on how the death penalty doesn't function as a deterrent, but instead, I looked at him and said, after a lengthy silence:

"I really feel a lot of energy from you on this question, and I feel you and I are on the same side because I think we are both very interested in reducing the violence in our society. I have a feeling that you've been really touched by crime yourself, or you've been in a job that has made you feel really burned by your experience. Would you explain why you have so much feeling?"

He responded that he'd had a job as a juvenile probation officer and then quit and went to law school because he couldn't cope with these kids who were so violent and so angry.

I said, "Wow, you've been in the fire and were burned. I respect you because I haven't had a job that was that hard."

This man's whole attitude changed. Tears were in his eyes. I went on to talk about how I want to prevent violence, that's why I volunteer with youth. I changed the whole debate from something dualistic and polarized to something where we could actually communicate in a constructive way.

I am able to respond this way by practicing mindful attention with people. I've come to realize that nothing really bad is going to happen if I take a deep breath and make deep eye contact with a questioner and actually draw him out more, whereas giving an answer actually stops the dialogue.

When the speaker is fully mindful of the group, her creativity is drawn forth to meet the needs of the audience. We are all connected, and if we stay present, we speak from this place of stillness, from the calm, loving presence of our hearts. We explore the intuitive voice that is always present, but often hidden from our conscious mind. We happen on inner truths just waiting to be discovered.

Transformational speakers have told me for years that they use speaking as a meditation:

> • "Being present fully in the moment—here and now, as speaker or listener—is vital to a soulful life. This practice has been a major force of light in my transformation process this year."
>
> • "The most important things for me are love, being genuine, and enjoying the support of the group. It was almost a mystical feeling. It proves that we have abilities and functions that we didn't know existed."

Listening with Soft Eyes

Listening attentively, with soft, "available" eyes, makes conversations with any number of people more enjoyable and connecting. Listening that way opens you up to receive others graciously.

Katherine belongs to a club that meets monthly. An overbearing woman started to attend meetings; she is opinionated and dogmatic when she speaks. In response, Katherine did not want to make eye contact, or give her any attention whatsoever, and she seriously considered leaving the club.

"To my surprise, at our last meeting, I found I could listen to her quite easily," says Katherine. "What makes the difference is imagining I am looking into soft available eyes, while returning soft available attention. Doing this, I instantly feel myself relax, and a gateway opens through which genuine words and connections flow."

This is a natural extension of speaking into support in a safe cocoon where fears meet the alchemy of soft available eyes—and are transformed into glorious, magnificent, authentic expressions of our truest, creative selves. The joy of rapt attention, and a sense of purpose and pure creativity, are possible, and portable.

"Listening Circles"

Many people feel that they get at least as much value from listening as they do from speaking. One participant tells of watching a woman stand in silence for the entire five minutes of her allotted speaking time, just going from one person to the next, listening to them and receiving each person's presence without any words. "She had such deep listening and open acceptance. There was incredible bonding. I felt I knew her in ways that probably couldn't have come if she'd spent the whole time talking."

Our job as heart listeners is to put aside the petty, defensive parts of ourselves and simply *be* with people in an accepting and loving way. The good feelings we experience from doing this are intense and immediate.

These good feelings make it easier to practice this state in our everyday life. One listener described it this way: "Listening forces me to go to a higher self. If I'm feeling judgmental, sometimes I have to go to a different frequency to find something that's both honest and positive. I have to stretch at first—but then it's so much fun to see the good rather than be critical, I get so involved I forget when it's going to be *my* turn to speak! Then, I can take that higher listening and higher self into my life and business."

Another said, "What I get from that kind of listening is peace of mind. Just sitting back and letting go of judgment and expectation. Luxuriating in really accepting that person and being able to feel good about whatever he or she does—it's tremendously relaxing."

Listen *Before* You Speak

As we discussed in chapter 2, most of us have lived for years with an imprisoned "Inner Speaker." Even people experienced at speaking from the heart may have some residual anxiety when we get up to speak. Usually, our fear is that the audience will sit in judgment of us. We forget that most people hope we won't embarrass ourselves—as they're afraid *they* would embarrass themselves if they were in our shoes—and they look at us with at least some degree of support and goodwill.

That support is there for us to accept—or not. If a speaker doesn't pause to take it in before he speaks, but instead dives headlong into his script or into amenities like "Hiya, folks! How's everybody? It's great to be here!" it is as if he is holding a stop sign up to the group and saying, "No, thank you. I don't need your support. I can do this *myself.*"

This separates him from the audience, severely limits the rapport that he can establish with them—even if he does everything else right. The first thing he has said to the group is "Stay away! Don't connect with me."

Yet his actual words probably say something different from this. So the first thing he shows the audience is: they can't believe him. He isn't intentionally lying, but they know he's not authentic. They may also suspect that he doesn't respect them, in which case they may resent him. He has denied that he is vulnerable, which makes it impossible for *them* to be vulnerable. The relationship has started off with the wrong dynamic, and he will be working the rest of the time to "bring them along."

If, on the other hand, we stand still for at least one deep breath and take in that support before we start to speak, we have a relationship with these people before we even open our mouths—whether we are speaking in a boardroom, a church sanctuary, or over coffee.

Karilee Shames, author of *Energetic Approaches to Emotional Healing* (Delmar), did that kind of breathing one-on-one with clients but had never felt permission to do it as a speaker. Speaking seemed like a different arena. But now she is able to use her understanding of energy flow while in front of an audience. "Standing and breathing with them for a minute gives me a chance to ground myself and connect with my own intuitive guidance before I start talking," she says.

At first it can be uncomfortable to sit or stand in the silence and receive support rather than filling that void with our own words and energy. But if we fill up the space, there is no room for *them*. We have to give them a chance to come to us. When we let in their goodwill, we begin the relationship on an equal footing. We are all human beings together, we all need support, and we can all reach out to one another.

In that time of silence, we receive into our hearts the full support of the audience. We experience being the center of attention with no need to perform. We let people see our beauty, and we see theirs. We make soft eye contact with one individual, then another, and another. We don't look at "the group"; we look at individual people and make a connection.

When we connect with people on this heart level, an electric current is sparked. We feel the contact and get energized as the rapport washes through us.

Performance anxiety dissolves as we focus on these people, feel them, and breathe them in. We actually take a deep breath and imagine breathing in their support. The temptation to rush our words or our thoughts drops away. We stand patiently within this soulful connection.

This silence may last a few seconds, or a few minutes. We usually let it last at least five to ten seconds. (In Speaking Circles, people so relish this wonderful feeling of connection that they sometimes prefer to stand silently for their entire three-minute check-in.)

The three *B*s help us open up to our audience and explore their support:

1. Be still.
2. Be silent.
3. Be receptive.

One speaker tells how she stays open to the support: "The key for me is remembering that the audience wants to hear what I have to say, and wants to be included. That makes it so much easier."

This process shatters the old myth that to be compelling, speakers must give to their audiences—that the audience's reaction to them is based solely on the quality of what they put forward.

No, it is our *receptivity* that draws people to us. It is what we let them give *us,* rather than what we give to them. People love to have their gifts received. As we take in their support, we use it to energize our presence and our message, and send it back to them multiplied many times over. That is what makes them listen to and receive us.

"There's an outrageous stream of energy available from being the focus of a group's attention," says a minister. "When I let it in and speak within that stream, magic happens. I speak from my heart into their hearts."

The more deeply we listen to others, the better we can hear ourselves. Pausing to listen to our audience before we speak also gets us centered before we begin talking.

Sometimes it is even appropriate to let your audience talk first. A corporate trainer was the last speaker on a three-person panel discussing telemarketing techniques. She watched the listeners' eyes glaze over as the other two rattled off information.

"The whole audience was frowning because they weren't getting their questions answered or their needs met," she recalls. "When it was my turn, I looked right into their eyes and announced that I would begin by addressing their questions first, then talk about what has worked for me. They lit up! I let them tell me what they wanted to know, and they scribbled furiously when I answered." Afterward, people thanked her for being so direct and to the point, and for saving them from suffering through a totally boring seminar.

Listen *While* You Speak

Pausing silently to receive the audience's support before we speak creates a sacred ground for our talk. To keep that field of resonance with our audience—we have to keep listening to them. The more we keep noticing and receiving our audience as we speak, the more they will hear us.

We remember to slow down, and take in one person's support at a time. We move toward them and honor them, rather than distancing ourselves from them or trying to dominate them. We may pause as we speak. Not a "pregnant pause" for effect, but a pause in which to "hear" the support, take nourishment from it, let it build, and feed it back to the audience as passion. We listen to them listening to us and the energy keeps building.

"That circle of constant feedback is like reading and being read by the audience," says an attorney. "When I'm really on, that's what's happening. I have a challenge in this area because I tend to live in my head. It's the best feeling in the world to relax into my heart."

Listening to the audience as we speak also tells us if they are hearing everything we say. Or if we need to slow down so that they can take in more. Kevin Davis, sales trainer and author of *Getting Into Your Customer's Head,* notes that most salespeople have perfected a conventional four-step selling process. But studies show that today's customer is using an eight-step *buying* process. So most salespeople sell faster than customers are willing to buy. His conclusion is "Sell slower to sell more."

Speakers sometimes do the same thing. We talk faster than the audience can listen. And impart more information than they can absorb. We may need to slow down to be heard better. Davis says, "When I slowed down I expanded my presence—*and* my effectiveness."

When we're listening, we know exactly when and how to slow down.

Listen *After* You Speak

When we're finished speaking, we stand in front of the group and take in the applause they give us. We don't run down from the platform with a sideways wave, or refuse to make eye contact, or roll our eyes in mock denial that we were any good. We stand before them, open and receptive, taking in their appreciation and applause.

The first time people come to one of my Speaking Circles, I almost always have to send them back to the platform to listen to the audience's applause when they are finished speaking—because brushing off compliments and resisting praise is "good manners." But think about how this feels when you are sitting in the audience, trying to let the speaker know you appreciate them. It's no fun to be rebuffed.

One person in a professional speaker peer-support Speaking Circle said, "The applause is just like a hug, and we should be able to accept a well-intentioned hug."

Often the "window/mirror" notion helps people listen to the audience before, during, and after they speak.

Turn Your Mirror into a Window

Many speakers act as if they have a mirror between themselves and the audience. They can never really see the people sitting in front of them, because the mirror only reflects back their own image. All their attention is on themselves. No wonder they are self-conscious and try to cover it up with masks or performance styles.

The trick to listening to the audience before, during, and after we speak is to *turn that mirror into a window.* We let them see us, and focus our attention on them. The connection is sparked, and all of us are energized.

Turning the mirror into a window also works wonders to reduce stage fright and performance anxiety. If all we have to stare at is a mirror, it's almost impossible not to wonder if we're doing everything right, if we're giving enough, and if we're avoiding all the mistakes that fill our worst nightmares.

When all we can see is ourselves, the inner critic goes wild. Focusing our attention on the other side of the window relaxes us and gives us something else to think about.

A child counselor who speaks to national audiences says, "Before, I was so focused on where *I* was that I couldn't see where *they* were. Putting my attention on my listeners gave me the confidence to just get up there and be free-wheeling. I'd never done that before. The fear dissipated."

"Focusing on what's happening in our relationship to-gether—the audience and me—makes me relax about how I am doing," says a marketing representative. "Those people aren't just a blur now, a mass of people rather than individuals. Before, I was afraid of what they might think of me. But now I just notice what they're about. It sure takes the pressure off."

Receiving our audience through a window, rather than blocking them out with a mirror, lets them be part of the re-lationship. We start to see that receiving is really the same as giving. *There is no distinction between the energy coming in and the energy going out.* It's just connection. We start to trust the rela-tionship and move within its flow, like playing among the rain-bows from a crystal in sunlight.

"The best part is give and take with the audience," says a fi-nancial consultant. "We do the talk together, as if we're one. Their emotion, my emotion; their insight, my insight." Public speaking for him has become an occasion for breathing to-gether, sighing together, trembling together, and grinning to-gether in a celebration of acceptance, intimacy, and magic. "It's a circle of energy coming from them to me—*to* them, to me," he says. "I can see them through love instead of fear. They actually become the best way I see them."

Ann Weiser Cornell, teacher and author of *The Power of Fo-cusing: A Practical Guide to Emotional Self-Healing,* tells of a breakthrough in listening. As the incoming President of the Association of Humanistic Psychology, she was expected to give a fundraising talk at the annual conference, to an audience of more than five hundred. "I was dreading it," she remembers. "My strategy for surviving public speaking situations in the past had been to write the talk word for word and then memorize it so thoroughly that I could deliver it as if it weren't memorized. If I didn't do that, I felt awkward and self-critical, and afterward could only remember how many times I'd said 'um' and 'ah.' "

When Ann started practicing transformational speaking, she began feeling safe and confident as her ability to connect with an audience "in the moment" grew. She was especially impressed by the other speakers in her group. "They were just being present, being real, receiving the energy of the audience. And yet they were spellbinding." Her only doubt was whether the magic of our intimate support circle would translate to an auditorium filled with five hundred people. But she was willing to try.

By the time Ann gave her fundraising talk, she knew that people need to be received before they can hear you. So she stood and let the audience in before she said anything. Opening with a simple personal story that had meaning for her, she breathed, connected with individuals, talked to one at a time, paused to be sure they got it before moving on, and did not use notes.

"That was the most satisfying fundraising talk we'd had in years," she reports. "We received double the amount we had been expecting! And people came up to me afterward and said, 'I don't know what it is, but when you're up on stage, I relax.' "

Speaking in front of groups is now one of Ann's greatest

pleasures in life. "There is a flow of energy that seems to come into me from the group, energy which then flows back through me to them. My natural gifts as a communicator have been unblocked—and I'm convinced that all people have these gifts."

Listening Is Charismatic

Most people assume that charisma is a kind of sparkling confidence that only certain people can radiate. I believe charisma isn't something we project, but a way we listen.

When we receive other people's energy and support, we can't help but see their beauty. That makes *us* attractive—in the same way that a mother's face is beautiful when she looks lovingly at her baby. *Whatever we see in others is reflected in our face.* This kind of charisma can belong to almost anyone, and it can be rekindled at will.

One sales trainer practicing this kind of receptivity was surprised to see in a videotape of herself that she was actually somewhat dynamic when all she was doing was receiving. She says, "I used to think that no one really wanted to listen to me, that I was boring. But now I know that people not only are willing to listen to me, but actually *enjoy* my presence. Listening and receiving have become my keys to being 'real' as well as elegant in public."

She recently did a seminar for professional salespeople and was the last on the panel to speak. When she stood up, she began to pour out information as everyone else had done, but it felt very mechanical to her. She stopped about two minutes into it, put down her notes, and connected with the audience. "I just received their presence and spoke from my heart," she smiles. "They said I was 'captivating.' When I started over, it was like settling into a place of comfort and ease."

President John F. Kennedy was a master of this art. At his press conferences, he listened to people, was wholly present to what they said, and allowed us to share in his relationship with them. On the surface, it looked as if he was giving something out, but he was actually taking in the group's goodwill, fondness, and respect. In films of his speeches, you can see him pausing graciously to let the crowd's love wash over him. That's the kind of charisma that is available to all of us.

Explosive Listening

"Explosive listening," a variation of transformational listening, is a term coined by Michael Gahagan, general manager at radio station WZTR in Milwaukee, who attended a communication workshop I conducted at the Radio Advertising Bureau convention in Dallas. After twenty years in the business, he discovered a whole new way of listening and relating to customers. Here's what happened, in Michael's words:

> We had a client who had done a lot of business with us in the past, and then suddenly stopped buying from us. We tried a couple of different ways to find out what the problem was. I went down there, we changed sales reps, but we never really felt like we were getting the whole story—so we never knew how to get back into this client's good graces. We offered some solutions, but we were presenting into a vacuum because we didn't really know what the root problem was.
>
> So one day I went down there and said to this individual, "Why don't you tell me a little bit about what's changed your mind about us." He listed some of the things we'd already heard, so I just kept saying, "Okay, yes" and encouraging him to continue talking. At some

point, he said, "That's about it." I didn't say anything. He just kind of looked at me, and I still didn't say anything. Really, for about thirty seconds, I just didn't say anything.

And then he erupted! It was incredible the amount of stuff that came out. I think part of it was that he felt relaxed, and he felt comfortable because it was a very non-threatening way of listening. It was just like, "I'm here, talk to me." Well, now we're going to be able to give him what he needs and not what we *think* he needs.

That same "explosive" listening has helped me internally with my staff as well. Instead of telling them what *I* think they need, I ask them what *they* need! And sometimes that happens best when I just shut up and listen.

Michael now trains his sales staff not to beat down people's objections. If someone says, "I just can't afford to buy right now," they don't rush in to deny or fix the problem. Instead, they stay quiet and listen. Michael tells me that invariably, when the customer feels heard, he virtually explodes with the information Michael's people need to serve him and make the sale.

Transformational, or explosive, listening is the capacity to make others feel fully heard in our presence, and it is the million-dollar communications skill. This deep listening can be applied not just to sales presentations, but to one-on-one communication, customer relations, executive management, or employee training, meetings, team building, and morale building.

Explosive listening, like transformational speaking, cannot be taught with technique. But given the right experience, it can be *caught,* and then it just happens naturally. As a result of that convention in Dallas, and other such workshops I have done, sales teams around the country now begin their meetings with a two-minute "go-around" in which everyone gets to voice concerns and acknowledgments, and announce successes—or just receive attention and support. Businesses are finding that when salespeople start the day being fully heard and fully seen, even for two minutes, they are better able to go out and allow their *customers* to feel fully seen and heard! That's what each of us craves, and it's great for the bottom line.

Explosive listening even works in the news business. Robin Doussard, former *San Jose Mercury News* feature editor and current deputy editor of the *Orange County Register,* told me about a reporter who always got incredible quotes at accident scenes. He came back to the newsroom with hot stuff no one else could get, and colleagues began to suspect that he was making it up. Robin finally asked him what his secret was, what questions he asked. The reporter said, "I don't ask anything. I don't say anything. I just stand there and let them be, and I listen. When they feel heard, they pour their hearts out. They tell me everything. They just blurt it out."

A top salesperson told me he is better able to listen to clients now. He's not so quick to jump in with *his* stories while they're telling *their* stories. "I breathe with them when they are talking, and I can almost see them get more comfortable when I do that. In the past, I was driven by a fear that I wasn't good enough, and that drove me to a lot of extra chatter." He doesn't have to try so hard to convince people now that he feels stronger inside.

Practice Listening with the Third Ear
. . . .

We don't have to be sitting in a Speaking Circle to practice listening with the third ear. We can practice it every day, at
home and at work.

If a potential customer voices an objection like, "My cash
flow is just too low," we can resist the urge to jump in immediately to set the record straight, or talk them out of their
point of view. Instead, *we can let a silence fall.* We can show
them that we hear what they are saying, and that we see them
as real human beings who need time to work out a challenge.
When we listen to people on this deeper level, they usually
tell us what they really need so that we can serve them. (We'll
talk more about this kind of "explosive listening" in chapter 13.)

When we talk with loved ones—particularly about uncomfortable subjects—we can let them have their say before
we jump in with our good ideas. If they pause for breath, we
can give them a chance to start again before leaping into the
void and giving our perspective. When they feel heard by us,
they will feel safe to speak from a place of deeper truth.

Many transformational speakers have created support circles for their families or work groups. Before beginning a
meal, for instance, they might give each family member two
minutes of support and positive attention in which to share
anything he or she has to say. Children love it!

Listening to Life
. . . .

The best thing that listening teaches us is how valuable and
precious every human being is—and part of that is seeing our
own value and listening to our own inner voices.

"Listening from the heart has affected the way I see the world and every relationship I have," says a teacher. "I'm not just more present and receptive, I'm more empathetic. I have a greater respect for my own foibles."

Cathy Dana uses her listening skills in her work as a hypnotherapist, and also in her personal life:

> My son Max is four, and I give him this kind of listening and attention. My husband and I use it, too. When we have something to discuss, we give each other five minutes of complete, positive attention instead of just jumping in and defending our positions.
>
> I also belong to a mothers' group that tended to get a little competitive, with everybody vying for "air time." I used to sit thinking about what I was going to say and how to be heard, but one day I came in with low energy and decided, "I'll just go and listen." I enjoyed the group *much* more and I found that things to say popped up naturally, and that when I talked, they all turned to me and really listened!

Cathy, who has a black belt in aikido, adds, "To me, this kind of listening is like aikido. 'Ai' means harmony or love. 'Ki' is energy. 'Do' means way or technique. So aikido is a way of harmonizing energy—and so is transformational listening."

Here are some examples of how people have applied this kind of positive listening to difficult situations:

• Sylvia, a mother of three grown daughters and a grandmother with a successful career, was visited by her seventy-five-year-old mom, who failed to recognize her as a fully competent, independent adult. After enduring three days of negativity and criticism, Sylvia found herself becoming equally negative and critical. She caught herself being reactive, verging on uttering words she might later regret.

"At that moment I realized how absurd this was," she says. "And, instead of lashing out, I paused for a few seconds to look into her eyes and listen to who she really was under the fear. Then I gave her positive feedback. She was disarmed." When Sylvia didn't engage with or react to it, there was no power to her mom's negativity and she couldn't be manipulated by it.

When her mom got back home, she called her daughter and told her how much she appreciated her and her achievements. "This was a first!" says Sylvia.

When you listen to someone's negativity, but don't reflect it back, they have to go off and face it themselves. This gives them room for self-examination.

• Kirk is a CPA from a straight Type A business background. He had a volatile first marriage and regrets spending most of his life talking down to people. "Since I began to practice non-judgmental listening," he says, "I am learning to be receptive and open, rather than follow my own agenda all the time." His recent marriage to Juanita is harmonious and cooperative because he listens to her. She's a serious student who's having trouble in her history class because of a language barrier. "I made a conscious decision to listen to her instead of trying to solve her problems for her," he says. "My days as the world's greatest problem solver are over!"

When we do not react from habit, initial perceptions, or impulses, then feelings pass through us and we can act and live from a calm center.

Listening with our hearts broadens our world. An office manager says, "The world looks a particular way through *my* eyes, but if I listen I can also see it through *other people*'s eyes. This way of listening widens my view of life, and it has very broad applications—in business, and with friends and associates."

In the next chapter, we'll look at the natural consequence of listening—connecting with other people.

. . . .

Chapter 5

CONNECTION IS EVERYTHING:
DROPPING THE BARRIER BETWEEN
SPEAKER AND AUDIENCE

> "I'd turn red and completely
> melt down."
>
> •
>
> "I ended up a quivering mass
> of fright and simply couldn't
> communicate."
>
> •
>
> "I feel disconnected from my
> brain up there. Hello,
> nobody home."

We human beings love nothing more than connecting, heart and soul, with one another. These connections inspire, energize, and give purpose to our lives and work. Most of us have experienced this synergy on a personal level. Now business leaders are discovering the power of connection, and the futility of trying to produce significant results without it.

"We are getting to the point where it is no longer enough to entertain and inform," according to futurist and professional speaker Chuck Moyer. "It is, and will be, demanded of speakers that they contribute to making a positive, permanent change in the lives of their audiences. This can only be done through honing the audience relationship skill."

Grady Jim Robinson, professional speaker and award-winning storyteller in St. Louis, wrote about "The Re-Awakening of Soul in Speaking" in his publication, *The Mythmaker's Voice*.

> Your impact as a speaker lies not in something called content but in something called *connecting*. The game is communication—not information. Everybody has the same information, or it is easily accessible.
>
> A speaker does not walk to a microphone and give a speech. The speaker ignites an event within a context of *relationships*. When we lose sight of the context, the on-going process, the in-the-moment human dynamic, we are thinking in mechanistic and archaic frameworks.

Leaders can no longer simply stand in front of a room and tell people what to do. To make an impact, we need to forge a strong, heartfelt relationship with people. That means we have to be authentic and human with them. We have to let them in, so they will let our message in.

This is the very essence of transformational speaking. We work from the inside out. Our connection with others starts at the core of our being, and touches people at the core of *their* being. That's why it is so important for us to understand the dynamics of connection.

The Illusion of Separation

Einstein is credited with saying "The tragedy of human nature is the illusion of separation." We are all connected in some mysterious way. To our sorrow, we forget it.

When we remind people of this by gently connecting with them, the illusion of separation is broken and we all feel the light of our oneness. We are always happiest, and at our best, when we live in that light!

The purpose of speaking transformationally is to dissolve

the illusion of separation, and that's how we come to compel rapt attention every time we speak. We humans love to experience the truth behind the illusion, the connection behind the separation. We are inclined to listen to anyone who makes us remember.

Author Salli Rasberry puts it this way: "I'm less intimidated by the idea of being the one 'up in front' now that I've changed my approach to speaking. It's not me and them. It's *us,* and we're dancing together!"

Where Connection Happens

Connection happens in the heart. It happens when we are connected with ourselves, and speak from our passion into the hearts of others.

One professional speaker says:

> If I'm present with myself, I have less need to control the group and the outcome of the program. I'm more spontaneous if I really check in with myself, breathe, and settle into where I am. Then from my self, I make contact with my Self, the higher part of me that will be with the participants. Then I can be spontaneous and go where *they* need to go, rather than where I need to go. We're connected, and that's the only way I can give them anything.

When we are at home with ourselves, we give other people permission to be at home with themselves—to relax into an acceptance of exactly who they are today.

"I wanted more than anything just to speak to people in the moment, peacefully, from my heart, without thinking about what I was supposed to say," says a consultant for a Fortune

500 company. "The first time I got up and let myself feel that heart connection, it was amazing! I had never spoken in front of people from such a place of peace, clarity, truth, and love."

Patrick Donadio, one of the original members of the peer support Speaking Circle at the Ohio chapter of the National Speakers Association, has been a professional speaker and trainer involved with personal development, empowerment, and business communications for twelve years. He was getting great evaluations but not feeling as personally connected with audiences as he wanted to be. Sometimes he felt as if he was operating on autopilot. Learning to be real about his passion kicked his presentations into a whole new gear.

"I talk about things now that really matter to me," he says, "and people feel the difference. I talk about my mentally retarded sister, my creative and challenging two-year-old son, my spiritual life as a Christian. Telling personal stories is new for me, intimate and exciting. I love it and I get a much bigger, more enthusiastic response by making that connection."

Professional speaker and author Patti Hathaway, another member of the Ohio circle, says, "I used to get up and *blast* people with information. Now, with practice, I've learned to have a conversation that just happens to be with fifty or five hundred people. Afterwards, people tell me, 'It was like you were speaking directly to *me*.'"

Another benefit for Patti is that she now remembers who was in the audience. After a full-day workshop, people would come up to her and she'd think, "Were they here all day?" She didn't recognize them because she had only *scanned* the audience. "Now I'm looking right into their eyes, not just glancing but really connecting with individuals," she says, "and individuals in my audiences are the people who hire me for future talks!"

Besides better business, another by-product of this connection, Patti points out, is how much more fun it is to be spontaneous and truly present with your audience. Giving the same talk more than once is never boring when you're connected with your audience.

Professional speaker Susan Schubert, a third member of the Ohio circle, also reaps the rewards of connection after the talk is over. What she hears from her audiences is "It was so comfortable being with you, I really feel like I can be myself." So in addition to *her* being authentic, this way of speaking gives *them* license to be real. "What a novel experience for some people who've come out of environments where they're afraid to be honest, afraid to express themselves," she says.

Susan claims her platform authenticity comes through the practice of "learning to trust that I will be able to say the right things at the right time and in the right way, without being microprepared." And she extends that trust to the audience. "You have the rapport and the relationship with them to trust that they'll also do the right things. Together you create a shared envelope in which everyone has a degree of comfort and you are all learning together, including the presenter."

She notices the difference when she sees other speakers doing things the way she used to. When she sees that kind of control, she thinks, "Oh, this new way is so much fun, why would I ever go back to being so much in control?"

Each Connection Is Unique

Connections among people are like snowflakes: each one is unique. We all have a special way of being with one another that is different from our connection with anyone else, and different from our connection with each other at any other moment in time.

One woman said, "I could be the center of attention for five minutes and not say anything at all, and someone else could get up and not say anything at all—and it would be a completely different experience because we're two different people with two different sets of connections in two different times. That means I can't compete with anyone, because I am completely different. *I can only get more like me.*"

If we remember our own uniqueness—the uniqueness of each connection and the need to re-create those connections minute by minute—we will never lack for intimacy with loved ones or audiences.

Instant Rapport: Four Basic Steps to Connecting with Any Audience

Intimacy is a "be," not a "do"—but here are four basic "do's" that can dramatically enhance your "be," in a public speaking situation.

1. Stand with your feet planted into the center of the earth—and listen to your audience before you begin speaking.

Leave at least five to ten seconds of silence—at least one deep breath—so you can "arrive" before you start speaking, and open the door to connection with your audience. Receive their support. *If you really let yourself see their beauty, it will be reflected back to them in your eyes.*

Try standing still, even if it is uncomfortable at first. Being still gives your listeners a focus: you. Standing still also prevents you from using movement as a nervous cover-up.

You shouldn't feel as if you're frozen stiff—but if you absolutely can't begin your talk standing still, then movement may be a cover-up.

You will notice an elegance and sufficiency in standing still. You may find yourself mentally "moving out" toward people without actually moving your body. Later, when you've mastered standing still, you will find your own "dance"—your organic, natural movements on the platform.

These moments of "listening" to your audience, which we discussed in the previous chapter, are where you find your connection with them.

2. Speak clearly, from the heart, in short sentences.

Once you've established the connection by receiving your audience in silence, keep it going by speaking in a way that makes it easy for them to receive you.

Tell a true personal story that allows you to relive an anxiety, a challenge, or an inspiring moment—that in some way makes you vulnerable. Your story can be about a dream (even a nightmare) you woke up to this morning, an adventure you had trying to get there on time, a time you felt like a failure, or perhaps a turning point in your life that stirred your interest in your topic.

Let them know that you are a human being, just as they are. You're not hiding your fears from them, so they don't have to hide their fears from you. Give your story even more power by telling them what you learned from the event and linking it to why you are here today. (We'll talk more about your opening story in chapter 11.)

When you speak from your heart, people know it. I once was invited to speak to a group of travel agency executives, but they gave me the wrong directions and I arrived an hour late—right at 7:30 for a 7:30 speech. Normally, I like to get there in time to chat with people and find out something about the group.

But that night I arrived breathless and had to start speaking soon after I walked in the door. Instead of getting stressed, I just stood for a long time and received their support. When I felt the connection, I told them I'd wanted to arrive at 6:30 to find out more about them and about the travel agency business, but had gotten lost. They laughed with me. Then I just looked at them and asked, "Who *are* you!?" Again, they laughed because I clearly didn't have a clue, and was admitting it. And they paid rapt attention to me because they could tell the question was sincere. The talk flowed from there.

People would rather hear the truth than anything else we can tell them, and they can receive any message better if we speak clearly from our hearts. Whether we are presenting a budget or telling the kids to be home by ten, the words don't matter as much as our attitude. If we connect with the kids in a respectful way and let them know clearly why we want them home by ten, they're more likely to get the message.

Presenting the budget may not include any deep emotional sharing, but it's bound to be more pleasant for all concerned if we are real and human, and if we connect with people as we give them the numbers. It can't hurt, and it may be very helpful.

3. *Say every sentence into the eyes and heart of a human being in the audience.*

Many traditional presenters speak to "the group" rather than to individuals. Their eyes sweep the audience or focus on the back wall, but they do not engage real human beings. Their eye contact is superficial, usually for a fleeting moment ("eye service," I call it), so that they take in everyone but see no one. Sometimes their eyes seem to glaze over.

Remember that you are speaking to *human beings,* not just to "audience members." Each time you meet someone's eyes, speak into that person's heart. Open yourself to how it feels to be there with that person. Let him or her know how it feels to be there with them.

Magic happens when we speak from our connection with individuals.

4. Spend five to ten seconds of quality time with each listener before moving on to another.

The conventional speaker's practice is to make eye contact with as many people as possible for one or two seconds each. The larger the audience, the more these speakers fragment their energy. They feel pressure to scan and move, sweep and hurry—and often scurry around the stage in the process. This approach tends to be distracting, stressful, and *disconnecting,* both for the speaker and for the audience!

For eye contact to have impact, it needs to be at a deeper level. As speakers from the heart, we stand still and engage individuals for five seconds or more, "listening" to each person, making a point, and staying long enough to make sure the person has heard what we said. *The ideal is to engage each person we focus on 100 percent, not to contact 100 percent of the people.*

At first, some speakers are afraid that by engaging individuals for that long, they will exclude the rest of the audience. *Just the opposite is true.* Listeners feel more fully included and connected with us when we make deeper connections, even if we make fewer of them. The group values quality of connection more than quantity of contacts, so there is no need to "cover" everyone in the audience.

It's as if those people with whom we connect deeply are surrogates for the entire audience. Everyone else watches the connection and *participates* in it, even when our eyes are not on them. We are creating more than a connection between ourselves and that one person; we are connecting the whole audience with one another and creating a community that includes all of us.

For Arnold, a corporate trainer, learning to speak to one person at a time was a breakthrough. Although he had known it to be a good idea, and *thought* he practiced it, he learned from watching himself on videotape that he didn't really do it. He was a scanner. He watched that video and faced the truth about himself the day before he presented an all-day seminar to sixty people. Speaking in the new way, very distinctly to one person at a time, created a bond he'd never had with an audience before, and it's been there ever since.

"I used to present *to* people, and now I feel as if I'm talking *with* them," he marvels. "There's much less preperformance anxiety because I'm just going to talk to people. I can just hang out with somebody, finishing a complete thought, and that builds a relationship with the whole audience."

These four basic steps to instant rapport are just as powerful at home and at work as they are in front of a room.

The Power of Soft Eyes

When we look at individuals in the audience, we don't stare them down, "drill" them with our gaze, or make our eyes into high-beam headlights blazing out energy that demands to be returned.

Instead, we softly focus on the eyes of people in the audience. Some of us are uncomfortable at first with sustained eye connection, and with good reason. Our early experience with eye contact is often related to "power tripping"—to adults who tried to exert their influence over us in some way, often by telling us who we should be or denying who we were. We came to think of eye contact as a dangerous thing. It was!

With a partner, or with a group of three or more people who agree to support our essence, even just sitting around a table, we have a safe place to learn to relax our eyes again. We look out at our listeners and receive total support. We remember how that feels, and learn to enjoy and expect it. We practice it until it becomes second nature to open into "soft eyes" in front of any group.

The Distinction of *Available* Eyes

Even though connection is the goal, looking too hard for that connection can get in the way. You want to *invite* people to be with you, without the pressure of expectations.

By being neutrally available for whatever each person your gaze alights on has for you—be it avoidance, a blank stare, a dirty look, or a supportive twinkle—you are putting absolutely no pressure on them to alter their behavior. If you are open to available support but maintain no expectations as to where you'll find it, I can guarantee that you will convert the blank stares, the averted eyes, and even some of the dirty looks, to twinkly support, just by being neutrally available for it.

For some, this subtle distinction may be the key that fully opens the wondrous portals of transformational speaking to you. I hear people say, "I can't connect right away. It takes me a while to warm up and get them warmed up." *No!!! Be available right away no matter how you feel.* If your eyes are softly available to individuals before you say a word, without trying to change how you feel just as you don't try to change how *they* feel, connection will quickly occur on its own, and your feelings of tightness, tiredness, or disconnection will pass immediately.

"Riding the Beams"
. . . .

John W. Travis, M.D., studied transformational speaking and writes about "soft eyes."

> I avoided real eye contact until I was fifty-two years old. Now I'm hooked on it.
>
> In my family there was little contact, eyes or otherwise. I learned to live in my head because it was the safest place in the house.
>
> Out in the world, I learned to fake enough eye contact to pass, but it ranged from uncomfortable to terrifying. In the hundreds of talks, presentations, and workshops I gave, I scanned the audience and occasionally someone would catch my eye and I'd feel good, but mostly there was no eye contact.
>
> Through the practice of transformational speaking I have found a new kind of eye contact in which I am fully seen and heard by other people. It's like riding on beams

of energy that I had always before experienced as fearsome rays from which I had to protect myself.

In transformational speaking, we learn to "ride the beams" in a way that feels exalting to both speaker and audience.

An executive specializing in recruiting leaders was in the habit of just scanning the audience, moving quickly from person to person in an attempt to cover the whole room. He found that the practice of soft eye availability with one person at a time slowed him down and has completely revolutionized how he speaks: "I remember that these are real people and I now share things off the cuff I wouldn't have shared before in public. I've started doing that in my work and training, and have found that authenticity gives me a lot more rapport with my audiences—and more reaction from them."

David Bradwell, an economist and expert witness, agrees: "I make eye contact with individual jury members before responding to each question. Developing this real, human connection with even two or three jurors is all it takes to get the whole jury listening to what I say."

These jurors have often been hearing testimony for several weeks and as a result have gotten quite punchy by the time David takes the stand. So making his eyes available is really worthwhile if he wants to be understood.

He gives that same attention and "listening with the eyes" to cross-examining attorneys, who try all sorts of tactics to unsettle a witness hostile to their position: anger, sarcasm, entrapment games, and so on. "By not rising to that bait and by continuing to keep contact with them," says David, "I cut through the games and dramatically reduce the time they spend trying to trip me up. Even though the courtroom is a formal, adversarial setting, people still hunger for quality communication."

The Eyes Have It
. . . .

Here are some other examples of how people have applied the principle of soft-eye connection in their lives:

• Leslie, a senior editor for a Web site on parenting, has adapted soft-eye contact as an effective parenting technique. Trying to get herself and her six-year-old son out of the house in the morning for work and school, she would shout across the house at him: "Did you feed the dog? Did you brush your hair? Your teeth? Did you make the bed?" Ten minutes later nothing had been done. "Now," she says, "I look him in the eyes and say, 'Okay, this is what I need you to do right now.' This way, it's harder for him to weasel out of it."

• Lauren had been waiting tables for several years with excellent customer rapport and then she discovered a whole new level of connection. Now that she maintains soft eye contact for more than a fleeting second, she finds that people have beautiful eyes, and she comments on them. "I'm amazed it never hit me before how much deeper a connection I can have just by looking at them," she says. "The tips, which I always did well with, are even higher."

• Similarly, Joanie, a hair stylist, has amplified her connection with her customers. She used to talk to them in the mirror the whole time. Now, when they are telling her what they want her to do with their hair, or when she has something meaningful to say to them, she turns the chair slightly toward her, faces them directly, and maintains soft eye contact while she listens and while she speaks. "I enjoy these moments, and my customer return rate has increased," she says.

• Shauna credits soft-eye connection, along with receptive

listening, for getting her through the Harvard University admission process. With twenty thousand applications for two thousand spots, the interviewers ask loaded questions to eliminate candidates. "I took a deep breath to absorb each question before tackling it, and I'm sure this practice separated me from the other applicants," she says.

Her most crucial breath came when she was explaining the reasons she started a young feminist club at her high school and one of her interviewers interrupted: "I supported Women's Lib in the '70s but things have changed and I don't think it's necessary anymore." Then he asked, point blank, "So how does it feel to be at the tail end of a dying movement?" Says Shauna:

> I was about to scream at him! I don't know what I might have said if I responded right away, but I'm sure it wouldn't have gotten me into Harvard. Instead, I took an extra deep breath and looked deep into his eyes, where I noticed a little twinkle. I realized it was a test, that he was baiting me. So I took another deep breath and said, with a twinkle in *my* eye:
>
> "You know, it's so interesting that you say that, because in all the work I've done for feminism, I've found that the greatest threat to women gaining full equality is people who think that women are already completely equal."
>
> They were impressed. The other one said, "Good answer." I'm sure that's what got me into Harvard.

Are You a Dynamo or a Magnet?

· ·

When you increase the voltage to generate electricity with an audience, you are being a dynamo. When you allow the available electricity to emerge by *decreasing your resistance to an audience,* you are being a *magnet.*

We ultimately need both dynamic and magnetic elements in our presentation style, and it would be a helpful starting point to identify which pole comes more naturally to you. Dynamic speakers may predominate on speaking platforms, but it could be a mistake to emulate them because the vast majority of us are more naturally *magnetic.* Naturally magnetic speakers can allow their dynamic side to emerge at times, and naturally dynamic speakers can develop their

	Dynamo	Magnet
At best	Transfixes audiences	Transforms audiences
	Motivates	Inspires
Opens	With confidence	With receptivity
	Punching	Breathing
Use of silences	Pause for effect	Pause to connect
Use of humor	"Makes" people laugh	"Lets" people laugh
Primary strength	Performance	Presence
Primary state	Doing	Being
Priority activity	Talking to audience	Listening to audience
Charisma comes	From exuding energy	From attracting energy
Electricity flow	Pumping out	Decreasing resistance in
Functional role	Teacher	Equal
Content	Tends to be scripted	Tends to be fluid

magnetic side, for variety, but identifying your innate style will help you maximize your speaking potential. See the accompanying chart for aspects that distinguish each style.

Keep Coming Back

Sometimes, after a particularly scintillating talk at one of my Speaking Circles, I'll ask the speaker, "How was that for you?" and they'll indicate disappointment by saying something like "I kept losing connection with the audience and had to keep pulling myself back, over and over again." I point out that this very act of reconnecting again and again is what makes the talk sing! As flesh-and-blood human beings it is our natural state to come in and out of connection. Catching ourselves quickly when we are on automatic, or distracted, and coming back home to our audience is very refreshing for them.

Remember, 100 percent connection is an ideal to shoot for. We may never achieve it, but moving in that direction is what generates the electricity.

There's Only One Audience

There is really only one Audience. When we understand how to connect with that Audience, we don't have to reinvent the wheel each time we stand up in front of a group. That Relationship with Audience is fundamentally the same, no matter how different the people sitting before us are.

It is simply a matter of standing before them in a real and open way, listening to them, and receiving their support. Once we can do that with one audience, we can do it with *any* audience. And everything we say and do can come out of that connection spontaneously and organically.

What we say and do will look different every time, but the nature of the connection remains the same: receiving them and responding in the moment, and giving the priority to our relationship with them rather than to a script.

A great place to practice that give and take, that rhythm, that fluid connection, is in a dyad of two, or in a peer support Speaking Circle. (See chapter 19 for how to create your own.) *When we know how it feels to do this with a partner, or in a group of three to ten people, we know how it feels in a gathering of any size.*

We don't worry about what we're going to say, or how we're going to say it. We may know our opening story and what we want to accomplish with our talk, but we let much of it flow out of our relationship with the audience, and the chemistry between us. We can't plan everything that is going to happen, any more than we can plan what will happen in a conversation with a friend or business associate—but we know we can trust that chemistry, and our instincts about Relationship with Audience.

I once spoke to a group of twenty interior designers at their monthly luncheon meeting. They were quite involved with one another and their work, and didn't seem very interested in listening to the speaking coach standing at one end of their table—especially since lunch was served just as I stood up to talk. The meeting was being held in a fancy room decorated like a wine cellar, and much fine wine was flowing. I could feel a chasm opening wider and wider between them and me, until I found myself sitting down—as they were—picking up my fork, and speaking to them as I would have spoken at a dinner party.

The energy around the table changed instantly. I had their attention! They were listening to what I said, and immediately

I got them involved in the conversation by having them take turns receiving one another's support as they spoke for two minutes about their work.

Sitting down and engaging them on a more intimate level was instinctive. It came out of what I know about Relationship with Audience. Just as I wouldn't stand talking to one person if he or she were sitting down, I knew that *I had to become one of them.* I had to get on their level, quite literally. I had to stop being The Speaker, and show my interest in *them.*

Larger Connection: The Community of Transformational Speakers

When people connect from their hearts and souls to share their truths, *community* is a natural outcome. It's a collective force of support, of shared vulnerability, and of people having the courage to stand in their own light and shine it on others.

In the process of discovering our own uniqueness, we also realize that we are very much alike. A professional speaker told me, "Transformational speaking offers a window to some values we don't always see in our society. We share things that are interior, not mundane surface stuff, and we have empathy with one another. That broadens and deepens my world."

Connection with other people is what human beings want more than anything. We desperately desire to shatter the illusion of separateness, and that is what we do in transformational speaking. One thing that makes that possible is "vibrant vulnerability," the subject of the next chapter.

. . . .

Chapter 6

VIBRANT VULNERABILITY:

THE WISDOM OF NOT KNOWING

When we let ourselves be vulnerable and embrace whatever we are feeling in the moment, we become vibrant and magnetic.

In fact, the more accessible we become, the more the audience is drawn to us and supports us. We aren't setting ourselves up as someone wiser, better, or smoother than they are. Our vulnerability allows them to show their vulnerability. We're all just human beings together, and we're enjoying it.

Hypnotherapist Marilyn Gordon,

> "I feel myself contracting in front of people."
>
> •
>
> "I can't catch my breath and I keep forcing myself to swallow."
>
> •
>
> "I have difficulty finishing even one sentence, let alone getting across what is really in my heart."

author of *Healing Is Remembering Who You Are,* had given a lot of talks about her work and techniques, but she'd always felt overprepared, overly organized, and wanted to speak more from her heart.

"I just wanted to let go," she says. "Transformational speaking unlocked something inside me so that I'm charged with loving energy and words just flow out of me. It's also taken away my stage fright!"

Now Marilyn shares these communication principles in her own group work with clients.

Training consultant Catherine Joseph wrote me after attending an all-day speaking workshop: "I've always tried to hide my vulnerability behind technique. The chance to stand before a group and to feel and show my vulnerability was both startling and scary. And yet I came away with an entirely different vision of myself as a speaker. I simply remember the joy of feeling scared but being lovingly supported by the group as I spoke."

People are always surprised at how powerful they get when they become vulnerable.

"Soft Power"
. . . .

Because speaking transformationally means never having to convince anyone that we are "right," we learn to stand "naked" before an audience in our truth, to reveal ourselves, and to stay open to our connection with them without the defenses we sometimes raise with people. This is what I call *"soft power."*

A minister says it this way: "To preach effectively, one must be genuinely present in simple, vulnerable humanity, connecting with the vulnerability in the audience. This builds an emotional network of communication and support, heals critical wounds, and empowers everybody."

Nervous Nirvana

· ·

Imagine turning nervousness and stage fright into a transcendent state that is actually exhilarating! That's just what graphic artist Charise Diamond did, and she called it "Nervous Nirvana."

Nervousness is just bottled-up excitement. When we're self-conscious about it and try to hide it, the nervousness gets worse. We get a "secondary nervousness," or *nervousness about being nervous,* that is uncomfortable both for us and for the audience.

When we just let our nervousness be, and perhaps even talk about it, it turns back into raw energy, radiance, enthusiasm—and even *ecstasy.* People who've suffered from terrible stage fright all their lives can finally say, "I've gotten through it for the first time!"

Charise Diamond

Nervous Nirvana

It all comes back to telling the truth, to speaking from our hearts instead of from our heads. As one career consultant says, "It's kind of hard to speak when the loudest sound is my heart. I remember the first time I spoke from here [my heart] instead of from up here [my head]. I saw that I didn't have to be so incredibly prepared in order to be successful." Now she doesn't know every word she's going to say, and if she's nervous she just lets herself be there.

"That ambiguity can be scary," she admits, "because I want to know how it's going to turn out, but the most moving thing I can tell them is where I am right now." She teaches people about job searches and allows that they do have to do some preparation, "but ultimately they have to trust where they are coming from and their ability to be themselves in the moment."

Your Magnetic Self

We usually avoid being vulnerable because, for whatever reason, we're afraid we aren't *enough*. We aren't smart enough, or charming enough, or informative enough, or inspiring enough. These are old messages, probably received in childhood, that have been playing in our heads for decades even though they have no basis in fact.

When we relax and open to our audiences, we become more *magnetic* than we ever could have imagined. Finding this magnetic self is just a question of letting the old tapes spin themselves out, exploring self-love and self-acceptance, and letting ourselves be vulnerable.

Saul Eisen is a professor and consultant. Although most of his teaching involves student participation, he also has to deliver lectures, and often speaks to nonacademic groups at conferences. An introvert, he generally hadn't been comfortable at these events, but then he had a breakthrough. He says, "I discovered a part of what I am naturally—introspective and thoughtful—that can work quite well as a speaker if I'm willing to be me while standing there in front of people."

When we're willing to be ourselves, even if we don't naturally look like what we think a "speaker" should look like, we become absolutely magnetic.

The Wisdom of Not Knowing

Life's adventure is in not knowing what's around the bend. The thrill of speaking comes when we don't know exactly what we're going to say, and let our words flow out of our relationship with the audience. Of course we know our subject and the basic points we want to cover, or the story we want to tell, but if our talk really comes out of our connection with the people in front of us, we can't know in advance exactly what we will say.

Not knowing can be scary. It's easy to feel five years old again and subject to ridicule or attack, to being ignored or put down. We have to trust our relationship with the audience and know that the right words will come.

As we practice "not knowing" in front of a supportive group, we find that the results are always better than what we could have imagined or planned. When this happens over and over, we learn to trust the process.

That's how transformational speakers are able to speak on the same subject again and again, and each time present a talk that is fresh, vibrant, and different from any other they've given. As much as half the talk comes out of the speaker's relationship with the audience, and the audience is never exactly the same. Letting them in allows the talk to take its own unique direction.

"If I'm willing to be out there without having it all together and knowing every word I'm going to say, then some amazing things come up," says a city planner.

"The biggest change for me is my willingness to drop into not knowing on the stage," confides a public relations specialist. "It's made me trust that something will come that both I and the audience need to hear. It blows me away that I start talking and an incredibly complete talk comes out!"

Instant Access

This willingness to "not know" in front of a supportive group pays dividends in public talks, where you *have* to know. Once we connect with our Inner Speaker, it quickly develops the agility to bypass our conscious mind and access what we know, when we need to know it. This means that as long as we know our subject and are committed to staying truly connected with our audience, we can prepare less and trust that the material will take care of itself.

A professional organizer says: "In the past I had to prepare a lot to speak in public because I'd be too nervous to think I could count on my expertise. Now, I just have an outline with key points. What allows me to be confident in accessing what I know is my connection with people. When I have rapport with the audience, it just flows."

Says a financial planner: "I am able to ramble in front of groups and figure out by gut feeling where I'm going as I go there. There's tremendous power in having no concern about your style. It strips away all the veneer and enriches the content."

A marketing consultant talks about a newfound ability to use virtually no notes and create new material on the spot: "This impromptu approach turns out better-quality material than anything I could have written. I somehow receive information, comments, and questions from the group and integrate them into the presentation without even thinking about any of it."

One writer has found that the less she prepares for a talk, the better it is. She can think about the subject, but the less she writes down, the more alive it becomes. "I flow with it and listen inwardly to what wants to be spoken," she says, "and I stand by that even when I think, 'Oh, these people can't hear *that* story.' People want to hear something real today. They need a certain form of nourishment that feeds the soul."

This same writer had a story about accessing material that bears telling here:

My father died this summer and in the middle of his dying I had to give a talk at a bookstore in another county. My whole focus was on him; there was no time to prepare or to know what to say. In that state you just don't care about yourself, or think of how to protect yourself, so there were no obstructions to speaking authentically. I just spoke without caring what people thought of me. I was supposed to talk about my book but I didn't mention it at all. It just didn't matter.

After I spoke, people told stories they'd never told before to anyone, and they shared secret dreams that were full of wonder. It showed me how important it is to be true to the heart because it knows what to say at any given time. Nearly everyone bought a copy of the book.

Layers and layers usually protect us from speaking from this very vulnerable place. But sometimes we are blessed by having the layers unpeeled and can come to trust ourselves more and more.

"White Space" Is Your Friend

Have you noticed that when three or more people are chatting and the room goes silent, many folks feel a compulsion to jump in and fill up the space? Professional speaker and media consultant Bob McCafferty, onetime anchorman and reporter at KXTV, the CBS affiliate in Sacramento, California, thinks that the awkward relationship with silence in our culture is partly a result of watching so much television. "The mortal enemy in broadcasting is dead air," he says, "so you always want to fill up the space. Now I am much more conscious of not trying to squeeze in 100 words where 50 would fit in conversation, or from the platform."

Now that Bob allows natural silences into his speeches, his evaluations include comments like, "Thank you for giving me time to think and to absorb the information." He also reports that these natural silences have crept into his life and made him a much better listener. He says, "My four adult children have remarked that they feel like dad listens more. There's nothing better than hearing that from your kids."

Jeff Rubin, who owns a full-service newsletter publishing company, Put It In Writing, says, "Many speakers have cluttered presentations because they don't pause. They seem to have this need to fill every available moment with sound. I find these speakers very hard to listen to." Jeff teaches that "white space is your friend." On paper it draws a reader's attention to what *is* on the page. When a document is cluttered, the eye doesn't know where to look first. Pausing and breathing in the white space spells successful communication in all media.

Allowing natural silence in a talk is the equivalent to leaving white space in a well-designed printed document. Whenever you pause in the course of a talk, you give your listeners a chance to refocus their attention. It's a very simple equation—less clutter, more focus.

Natural silence is also very good for relationships. When Phil Blagg left his job as a firefighter and moved into a small cabin in Nevada with his wife, Beverly, issues of intimacy could no longer be avoided. With nothing to distract them from the building tension, they both found themselves able to lovingly express the truth without hurting each other. During moments of fear and not knowing, instead of arguing back and forth or talking about what they were thinking, they discovered a new ally: silence.

"In the past I had equated someone's silence, or lack of immediate response, with disapproval," says Phil. "But I discovered a silence that allows Bev to fully integrate what she is hearing from me before she formulates a response. And in that same silence I am able to be calm, quiet, receptive, and listen to what I have just said as well." Even when they disagree they can feel each other's support. They trust the silence.

"I could talk all day about the value of silence," says Phil, grinning.

The Power of the Dreaded "Lull"

. . . .

Some speakers panic if a few seconds pass in silence. The void just makes them feel too vulnerable. They rush in, saying anything just to end the silence. Or they finish making an important point, and rush right on to the next point without giving the audience a chance to digest the last one.

When we talk with people we love, we don't work to fill in the silences. Those silences feel comfortable. They give us time to absorb what people have said, to let things sink in, to think, and to just quietly enjoy one another's company.

It's important to let ourselves experience the vulnerability and power of natural silence for three reasons:

1. When we move from point to point without stopping to breathe, our listeners can get breathless.

They lose focus, have trouble concentrating, and may miss what we say because there isn't enough time for our words to sink in.

2. If we allow the silence, and even sustain it, we can see whether or not people are taking in what we say.

We need to know if they are not following what we say, so that we won't just blaze forward and leave them even farther behind.

3. When we're not sure what to say next, it's important to relax, take a deep breath, and wait in the silence until the right words come.

This is far better than rushing ahead with something that isn't right, and pushing the whole talk in the wrong direction. When people talk about "thinking on their feet," they often imagine that this will save them from those awkward silences. Just the opposite is true. Presenters who "think on their feet" are usually those who don't mind silence. It's their ability to relax into a natural silence that lets them think on their feet so well.

When we're not comfortable with silence, then much of what we say comes from fear of silence—whether we are with one other person or a thousand people. Think of a time when you were with another person who couldn't stop talking, who refused to let a silence fall. Chances are, you didn't feel that person was coming from the deepest place within himself.

The old speaking paradigm was about *breaking* the silence; in transformational speaking, we *come from* the silence. We begin with a comfortable, accepting, silent connection, and let everything we say come out of this connection.

When Marlyn Jenvey, a Certified Financial Planner, started opening her talks with a few deep breaths before plunging into her material, she began to notice the colors people were wearing. "That was the fluid beginning of the rapport I now have with groups," she says. Now that she takes the time to look at each participant, she has a newfound ability to tailor her information to her audience on the spur of the moment. Honoring the natural silences allows her the receptivity to really listen to their questions. Then she can relax into the choice of asking for more information rather than jumping to answer the question right off.

"I don't rush to respond. A little silence is okay. In fact, a few seconds of silence can make a huge difference. I didn't have the flexibility to do that in the years I concentrated on the syllabus, my material, my plan—my *fantasy*—for how I thought the class would go."

As a community leader says: "When you get out of the way, your heart and mind know what to say and how to say it."

Drawing a Blank

. . . .

Fear of drawing a blank is related to the fear of silence—and we can use the same antidote. We can simply stop, allow ourselves to be vulnerable, and let the silence be. We can give the problem a chance to solve itself.

If we relax, the right words come. In the silence, we breathe in the group's support, stay connected with people, and resist the temptation to rush. Almost always, the audience believes our silence is intentional.

If we start to forget our material when giving a "real" speech, we can always walk over to our notes on the lectern. We can take a sip of water, and give ourselves some time. If we have a script, we can refer to it.

We can even ask the audience, "Where was I?" I've heard speakers ask this, and the audience leaps to help. We've been taught that drawing a blank is a bad thing, but this is one of many ways it can be turned to our advantage.

A corporate trainer says, "When I draw a blank now it's not a blank of fear, it's a blank of openness, and it doesn't last for long. I used to have to script everything because of my fear of drawing a blank. Without that concern, the material emerges naturally and fits any amount of time I have been given."

"My greatest fear had been standing up in front of an audience and not having anything to say, or not being able to speak," said a writer. "Now I can tolerate the unknown. I have found that silence can speak, too."

Sometimes we draw a blank because our talk was headed in a direction that wasn't working very well, and we knew intuitively to stop. Or perhaps we had become a little automatic in our presentation, and finding ourselves in the void was a chance to reach out creatively to connect with the audience.

One of my clients tells the story of attending the symphony in San Jose to hear a famous piano soloist. A few minutes into one piece, the soloist knew that something was wrong. He stopped playing and called the conductor over. After their consultation, the conductor announced, "We're gonna start this one over again."

The audience loved that, and their response was thunderous. They empathized with the soloist as he passed through the ultimate fear of failure, literally stopped the music, shared his feelings with them, and lived through the experience. Consciously or unconsciously, they realized that he'd shared with them a life lesson that went beyond good music.

Journalist Gregg Levoy, author of *Callings: Finding and Following an Authentic Life* (Harmony), tells a story about the vulnerability of drawing a blank, and what it taught him. He was always good at teaching and lecturing, but wasn't confident that he could do it without notes. "Getting caught without my notes was my worst nightmare," he confides.

A few years after he was introduced to transformational speaking, Gregg was about to teach his first class as a professor at the University of New Mexico. He stepped to the front of the room, opened his briefcase, and suddenly realized he'd left all his notes at home. He looked up over the top of his briefcase at a class of forty people, panicked, then flashed back to his transformational speaking experience.

"I knew this material. I had been living it for years. I could do this if I just told them what I knew. That turned out to be one of the best classes I'd ever had, and a breakthrough. I can just be there and be vulnerable, and it's still going to turn out all right." For Gregg it was a life lesson as well as a speaking lesson.

Once we get past our fear of drawing a blank, it will never

again be a problem. We become committed to "say no line be-fore its time."

Vulnerability: The Hero's Journey

One of the most courageous things we can do is stand before a group of people we don't know, without pretenses or de-fenses, and allow a relationship to develop out of our vul-nerability. That shows us more about ourselves than almost anything we could do. It is a heroic act, and people appreciate it. That's why vibrant vulnerability elicits such strong sup-port.

Here is what some speakers have said about their hero's journey.

• "I love hitting that spot at the bottom of me where there seems to be a void, but it's really like the depths of the ocean where all the nutrients are. All the good stuff bub-bles up from the bottom, from the emptiness. In that emptiness is a fullness."

• "Oddly, being vulnerable gave me a sense of presence and confidence. I used to feel competitive and would want to appear to be a certain way when I spoke. Sometimes I still collapse into those defense systems when I'm flus-tered, but I'm more and more willing to be out there with-out the need to impress, arm myself against pain, or shape myself into something I'm not. Instead, I become who I am, and that makes it fun."

Vulnerability Is Contagious

. . . .

Not only does the speaker often feel obligated to fulfill a role, the audience often feels that way, too. Opening up in front of a group allows your listeners to open up, too. Both parties' vulnerability breaks down the prescribed roles of "performer" and "audience" so that everyone becomes part of one whole.

Karen Clark Edmiston, M.A., speaks to women prisoners about growing up in extremely dysfunctional families. She says:

> You walk into a room with eighty convicted felons with sentences from six months to life and you see in front of you what you would anticipate seeing, based on movies: flat affect, a hard cold edge, khaki clothes, a lot of attitude, body language that says "You're just another one of those authority figures, I'm not gonna trust you."

With the heavy peer pressure to maintain their roles within the prison family, along with their hostile attitudes, these women do not reach out to psychiatrists and counselors within the system. Karen has found that the only way to gain their trust and allow them to feel safe enough to participate is to speak, sometimes for as long as an hour, with tremendous vulnerability.

Typically, one of the women will finally raise her hand and crack the wall of separation with words such as "I don't know how I will ever recover from the guilt I feel for what I've done to my children. I left my little boy when he was six months old and he'll be twenty-two when I come home."

At that point, Karen reports, there is a chain reaction of sobbing, hands going up, people saying what they need to say.

"It is a domino effect, where one person speaks the truth and suddenly the whole room is filled with honest emotion instead of what people assume a prison room would be filled with." The best part for Karen is seeing lives turn around: "Hope does return. Freedom and release come out of speaking the truth. But someone needs to stand up first and model vulnerability."

Transformational speakers find that vulnerability can be our greatest strength. But what can we do when we feel overwhelmed by stage fright? The next chapter contains some sure fire solutions.

. . . .

Chapter 7

EMBRACING FEAR:

SHED "THE SHAKES" AND

END YOUR STAGE FRIGHT FOREVER

We can tap into our wondrous Inner Speaker, learn to let go, to be authentic. We can listen with our heart, we can achieve connection and rapport, and our vibrant vulnerability can make us truly magnetic. But what about those times when our vulnerability seems to slip over the edge and we feel paralyzed with stage fright?

> "I am terribly anxious in front of groups, always inwardly scrambling and trying to think of what to say, my eyes darting all over the place."
>
> •
>
> "I'm an introvert, not a performer. In college speech class I threw up after every speech."
>
> •
>
> "My hands shake, my palms sweat, and I can't hear myself speak."

Embracing fear is the next step in transformational speaking. We can move from stage fright to grace using our basic tools of authenticity, support, listening, and connection—plus a few secrets we'll discuss in this chapter.

Stage fright is nothing more than the fear of speaking our own truth and being judged. Transformational speaking gives us the tools to deal with that—whether the occasion is a speech, an interview, a performance evaluation, a marriage proposal, an important presentation to a potential client, that first meeting with your in-laws, a difficult communication to a friend, or the first day on a new job.

Our Biggest Fear, and Where It Comes From

We are a nation of people with stage fright. We've already seen that public speaking is the number one fear among Americans—it's even more frightening than death! Comedian Jerry Seinfeld quotes this fact and concludes that at a funeral, most of us would rather be in the coffin than delivering the eulogy.

We also know that stage fright comes from early wounds. As children, we were either punished or made to feel embarrassed or ashamed for being ourselves, so we stopped trusting ourselves to speak and act in acceptable ways. We began editing ourselves and living in fear of making the same kind of "stupid" mistakes again—especially in public. Chapter 5 was about healing this wound and reclaiming our Inner Speaker. This chapter is about what to do in those odd moments when terror sneaks back onstage with us.

Stage fright generally shows up as fear of two rather daunting phenomena:

1. The black hole.

In the black hole, we draw a complete blank and have nothing to say. We stand, paralyzed and speechless, before an audience of three, ten, fifty, or thousands of people. Seconds drag into minutes, and still no words come. Eventually, the audience slowly gets up and leaves. That's the nightmare, the fear. It has nothing to do with reality.

I invite people to practice letting themselves fall into the black hole, to sit with a supportive individual or to stand in front of a supportive group with nothing to say. Once they've had that experience, this fear rarely recurs in full force. They survived the thing they dreaded most, so they no longer fear it.

2. The family of a thousand.

As mentioned before, we tend to look out into the audience and see not friendly co-workers, pleasant strangers, or interested potential clients, but *a room full of disapproving, reprimanding, ridiculing, snickering family members.* We are two years old, starting to express ourselves in the world, and getting shot down. Or twelve years old and destroyed by a critical teacher or disapproving peers. We're ignored, heckled, sometimes even physically attacked.

Stage fright can be so severe that people turn to drastic solutions—most of which don't work.

Fear Band-Aids
. . . .

Almost everybody gets stage fright—even seasoned professional speakers. Many of them learn to bulldoze through the fear with bravado, or to cover it up with "professional techniques," fancy footwork, and exacting preparation, but this usually keeps them from really connecting with the audience. If the speaker is putting up a front, the audience has to put up a front as well.

Many traditional public speaking gimmicks are nothing but fear *Band-Aids.* Since childhood, Fredrick remembers, the formula for speaking in public had been to look at a spot in the back of the room, such as a blemish on the wall or a picture, just over people's heads. "Not looking at the people I was speaking to—or at—got the job done, got the information imparted," he says, "but it sure didn't feel comfortable or sound natural. When I practiced forcing myself to make eye contact with people rather than making a connection with a paint fleck, I finally got the support I needed to be *myself.*"

For four years, before presentations, Charlotte Melleno took beta blockers, a popular drug that works on the autonomic nervous system cutting off all physical sensation of anxiety by stopping the flow of adrenalin. It eased her fight-or-flight response—her dry mouth, sweaty palms, and shakes. This, in turn, relieved her anxiety about how she looked to the audience.

"The down side," says Charlotte, "is that they flatten out your voice and emotions." Then she learned to relieve her stress the natural way, by connecting with her audience, and she reports that in her next talk "I felt involved, vivacious, interested in the people, like we were having a conversation. They were visibly moved and their evaluations were exceptionally positive. I'll never use beta blockers again."

These Fear Band-Aids are not the answer to stage fright. At heart, speakers who use them are usually still scared. When something goes wrong or something unexpected happens, their composure slips. Even when nothing goes wrong, listeners sense that something is missing. It's as if the speaker is not really live, but on tape. This type of act is wearing thin in today's marketplace, and will wear out completely in the marketplace of the future, as people become less and less likely to trust a polished facade.

Being willing to let others see where we are emotionally, even when we're scared, defines an authentic relationship. But speakers who depend on "holding it all together" are terrified of this prospect and are apt to reach for a Fear Band-Aid instead.

What to Do: Embrace the Shakes

There is nothing shameful about being afraid of public speaking. Everyone in the audience has experienced it, and they are thankful that we're standing up in front instead of them. If we can stay with the fear and move through it, we act as *surrogates* for them. We are conquering their past and future stage fright for them, right before their eyes, and they appreciate it.

If we avoid resisting or hiding the fear, it can actually bond us to the audience. Transformational speaking teaches us to notice, accept, and respect our fear. That stretches us, and the audience knows it. They're rooting for us.

To move beyond stage fright organically, naturally, honestly, and in a way that builds connection with the audience, we simply stand before them and feel the fear. In a support group, we might talk about it. In a public speaking situation, we probably wouldn't. But in any case, we need to keep breathing in their support. That support grows with every second, letting us reach more deeply into our own wisdom, and we start to feel more at ease. As the electricity builds between ourselves and the audience, we feel more relaxed and focused on why we are there. Of course, all of this is much easier if we have practiced it well in a support group.

Jan Mundo, a somatic therapist who specializes in the relief and prevention of chronic pain, suffered tremendous fear of speaking in front of groups of even three or four people. Her symptoms included frozen movements, a tight throat, heart palpitations, the works. She wanted to expand her teaching of headache relief to lecture and workshop formats, but the fear was keeping her back. She attended a Speaking Circle and was so nervous she could hardly stand. She found herself sitting down on the floor, where she began receiving people's attention and looking into their eyes. She remembers:

A magical transformation happened where we had a conversation without speaking a word. Then I told them I was scared. Later, the feedback was that they felt they were looking into my soul and that I was beautiful. This experience was extremely profound for me—to have exposed my fear to these people and not be seen as ugly or weak. That single experience increased my ability to talk to a group of three or three hundred.

Now Jan does quite a bit of public speaking and has the same kind of ease in being herself that she had performing in stage productions in her youth.

Receiving Makes Us Strong

Focusing our attention on others almost always relieves stress, and this is particularly true in public speaking. When we focus on receiving the people in front of us, we naturally become less self-conscious. The more we put our attention on them, the more comfortable and confident we feel.

One trainer was a wreck because she was always thinking, "What am I going to say? How am I going to come off? How am I going to do?" The first thing she does now is remind herself that there are real people out there, people she wants to honor and attend to. *She takes a few moments to really look at them and take in their support.* Even if she feels shut down, she opens up to receive them. This changes everything. "In that moment," she says, "I'm more deeply connected to them than I often am to my co-workers or friends. There's so much satisfaction in connecting with people from that heart place that it doesn't matter if I'm nervous."

"Stage fright? I was the poster boy," says a successful professional speaker and entertainer. "I always felt nervous, with a dry mouth, having to pee, shaking, forgetful. But there's a part of me now that's just eager to get out there and connect. The excitement and anticipation are greater than the fear."

It's a little like the anxiety an athlete feels before the big game—a little nervous from all the raw energy, but full of anticipation, waiting to pour that energy into the moment of truth.

"I used to rely on the content of the talk as my security blanket and focus on delivering the information," said an advertising executive. "But I'm a lot more comfortable now that I concentrate on the relationship with the audience."

Defusing the Inner Critic

The Inner Speaker always competes with the Inner Critic. The Inner Critic is that negative voice within us that constantly criticizes us or puts us down. When we're in front of the room, the Inner Critic sits on our shoulder, judging everything we say and do. Each of us has a tailor-made version of this little heckler who points directly at our most secret imperfections, and aims his taunts at precisely the weaknesses we most want to conceal from others.

We don't want to kill off the Inner Critic. It is just one of many voices within us, and can actually be helpful at times. The Inner Critic keeps us from screaming at inappropriate moments, throwing food on the wall, or performing other embarrassing acts.

The best way to work with the Inner Critic is to let it have its say—but not to let it have the final say, and not to take every word it utters as the truth. Fighting the Inner Critic only makes it stronger and feeds it power. We need to accept the Inner Critic, but not take it too seriously or let it run the show.

When we're in front of the room, we can let the Inner Critic jabber away without paying too much attention to it. It becomes like the background noise of a television that nobody's really watching.

Remember: it's not the crime, it's the cover-up. It's not the Inner Critic that's so terrible; it's that we're denying it, judging it, embarrassed by it, or trying to cover it up. The problem is not the Inner Critic, it's our inner criticism of the Inner Critic.

Even when there's some truth to what the Inner Critic is saying, we have to remember that it has a very narrow perspective. Maybe we *would* look better without those twenty pounds, but that doesn't mean people aren't going to be moved and inspired by what we say. Maybe we could have prepared more, but perhaps people can only take in as much as we brought with us today. Maybe we aren't as charming as our baby sister, but perhaps charm isn't the best quality to bring to this particular material.

The Inner Critic also tries to get our attention *after* we speak—and we can use the same antidotes. A writer and consultant told me:

> I gave a talk about advertising at one of those high-tech luncheons. It was pretty good, but right in the middle, I lost my train of thought. The great feeling that I love in talks, the connection, broke momentarily. Probably nobody noticed, but on the way home, that was the only thing I could think of. My focus was not on the fifty-nine minutes when I was doing a good job. It was on the ten seconds when I felt I lost control.

As we begin to notice how our critic works, we can move its voice into the "background noise" and start feeding the positive aspects of ourselves with attention. When we humor and embrace the Inner Critic without giving it power, and keep what it says in perspective, then we will always be superior to it.

"I used to listen to the screeching, judgmental voices of my internal nit-pickers, filling my head with negativity as I tried to speak," says singer and songwriter Jana Stanfield. "It is a joy to hear, instead, a gentle affirming voice filling my heart with courage . . . and I can now quiet an audience of rowdy teenagers without saying a word."

The Inner Critic Gets Lonely and Slinks Off

The best way I know to defuse the Inner Critic is by practicing with a friend or in front of a supportive group. Positive feedback makes the Inner Critic very quiet. As one accountant says, "In an environment of absolute support, my inner critic gets very lonely." Nobody else in the room validates it, because there is nothing voiced but support and positive acknowledgment.

The Inner Critic gets even lonelier when we have an opportunity to watch videotapes of ourselves, and see the beauty that emerges when we come out into the group's support. The Inner Critic may be pretty noisy the first time we watch our tapes. "See?! You're fat! You're tongue-tied! You don't know what to do with your hands!"

But by the second and third time we watch a tape, the other voices have their turn. We can't deny that there is connection, warmth, and bottom-line lovability. No matter how many times the Inner Critic jumps up and down screaming

"You're bad, you're bad, you're bad," we can see with our own eyes that it's just not true. That helps us take everything the Inner Critic says in the future with a grain of salt.

Grant Flint had a sixty-year history of chronic stage fright. The first time in his life he was able to be himself with others was at a Speaking Circle:

> I hadn't done that with my wives, children, or closest friends. It was a chance to experiment with positive feedback, to explore the various aspects and contradictions in myself, to be completely open and vulnerable in a safe setting.
>
> As a speaker, *all* audiences seem friendly to me now. I connect easily one-on-one with members of any audience. I feel more honest, humble, vulnerable—human and intimate—with the people I speak to. My stage fright is 10 percent—my delight in being onstage being myself, loving people, and being loved is 90 percent. And my secret extrovert has come out of the closet. Being myself is everything.

Easy Acts to Follow

It is common for a newcomer to my workshop, when called upon to take center stage after someone else's particularly wonderful talk, to start by muttering glumly, "That's a tough act to follow." This line inspires a groan from the regulars, who have come to understand its self-defeating absurdity. And they know it's the one line that I, as facilitator, have trouble letting pass without an interruption and a lecture that breaks my own rules.

"That's a tough act to follow" comes from the competitive

Inner Critic at its most devious and cunning. In fact, the audience is making no such comparison. If they are enchanted by one speaker being exactly who *he* is, they are that much more ready for the next speaker to be exactly who *she* is.

I learned this lesson in the innocent days of the San Francisco stand-up comedy scene in the late 1970s, when I was a perspiring comedian hiding behind my jokes. "That's a tough act to follow" was our predominant mind-set. Most of us dreaded following a great set—as few and far between as they were in those days.

Then a new comic named Robin Williams showed up and broke the mold. I was there for his first "open mike" opportunity, and the audience response gave no indication of how successful he would become. But he rooted for the rest of us, reveled in our victories, and within weeks found his stride. He seemed to love surfing the energy generated by the prior acts and taking it through the roof. He made us all better with his positive outlook.

I began to notice how hopeful and eager an audience looked when I followed someone who had uplifted them. *But I had to look.* If I didn't look, the Inner Critic turned a great advantage into a deficit by making irrational comparisons.

Transformational speakers come to root for each other without reservation, and we learn to love "surfing the stage" after it has been graced by a *tour de force*.

Look Before You Speak

The quickest turnaround I've ever seen from agony to ecstasy was at a workshop I conducted for psychotherapists who wanted to be better at speaking in public to market their practice. After sharing my ideas about transformational speaking with them, followed by a small circle exercise, I had a few participants address the entire group. Then I asked for a volunteer who had such severe stage fright they *dreaded* the thought of coming up, but knew they needed to move past this block to speak effectively about their practice.

A red-faced young woman rose and trembled to the front of the room, amazed and horrified that she had answered the call. I handed her the microphone and sat in the front row to coach. I said, "Look at us and just take in our support."

With eyes glued to the floor, she muttered, "I'm so scared."

I said, "No, please just look at us."

She lifted her eyes, they widened, and instantly a huge smile spread over her face as she said, "I'm not scared." From that point, her words flowed and her spirit soared.

In five seconds, she had experienced the subtle shift in focus that moved her past a lifetime of stage fright into a future of grace under pressure—the shift from anxiety about *giving* to relaxing into *receiving*.

Death, Taxes, and Stage Fright: Making Friends with Fear

Stage fright is a fact of life. It will always be with us, but it doesn't have to stop us from having a good time or from speaking effectively. We may always feel an undercurrent of timidity when we think of speaking in public, but we can take inspiration from Eleanor Roosevelt, who used to tell people, "It's all right to be shy, just don't let it get in the way of doing things."

Fear isn't something we get rid of, in speaking or in life. But we can make friends with fear. We can practice not letting it stop us or make us miserable. To help us, we have the strongest force in the universe: love. What lets us live with fear is the knowledge that we can rise above it through our connection with people.

A graphologist (handwriting expert) says:

> I used to try getting over my stage fright, but now I see that fear as a place to *explore*. A place where I can learn more about myself. I've made a lot of money in the past year and a half, testifying in court as an expert witness. Before I discovered transformational speaking, I would have let fear keep me from doing that. I'm also enjoying myself more at parties and family gatherings."

Making friends with stage fright is one of the most exciting things about transformational speaking. When we've done that, we can handle even the difficult audiences described in chapter 9.

THE LAUGHING SPIRIT:

HEALTHY HUMOR

"My knees shake so much, my pants are wearing out from the *inside*."

•

"I sweat so hard, I break out in *fish*."

•

"I feel like a clown, and my students don't waste a moment telling me I look like one, too."

We all have the Laughing Spirit. It comes from a place deep within us—a place of love, connection, and amusement at our predicament as human beings.

The Laughing Spirit is released whenever we break the "illusion of separation" and remind ourselves in a lighthearted way that we all share the same human foibles, and that we're all connected. My favorite Laughing Spirit joke is a riddle:

How do you make God laugh?

Tell him your plans.

We're all a little lost, if the truth be known, and the Laughing Spirit is able to make light of that fact and even make it an adventure. It acknowledges the chaos that lives within each of us. Scientists say that the order of the universe is chaos. I think that each of us is a universe of chaos. The Laughing Spirit addresses that.

People feel comfortable and relaxed around us when we can laugh gently at our own pretensions and be compassionate about the pretensions of others.

I believe that to fully invoke the Laughing Spirit in a room, the space must also feel safe enough for your listeners to *cry*. Laughter separated from tears falls flat, both on the ears and on the heart.

Three Kinds of Humor

Humor comes in three flavors. Each evokes a different kind of laughter: Laughter of the Head, Laughter of the Spleen, and Laughter of the Heart.

1. *Laughter of the Head*

Laughter of the Head is evoked by cleverness and wit. It often involves wordplay, irony, light jokes, or esoteric references and allusions. It's not harmful in small doses, but it tends to become competitive. One person plays off the last person's comment, and the conversation becomes a duel of intellects. It's a mode of humor that encourages one-upsmanship.

Head humor can keep people at a distance. We all know someone who feels compelled to be "on" all the time—but never shares very deeply and often doesn't say what he or she really means. No one else in that person's environment feels safe to share honest emotions or vulnerabilities, either.

Children are often "humor abused" with Laughter of the Head. A six-year-old says at the dinner table, "I want to be a fireman when I grow up." His father fires back, "Well then you can start by hosing down the dishes in the sink." It's funny and draws a laugh, but the little boy doesn't get the joke. He just feels defeated, confused, and mildly put down—and he may disappear into himself.

From the platform, clever lines may win the battle for laughs but lose the peace in our audience's hearts—and hearts are what move minds and bodies to action.

The old conventional wisdom for speakers was to open with a joke, and it usually involved Laughter of the Head. A speaker on health might say, "Did you hear about recent studies showing an increase in heart disease in China? I'm not surprised, with all those Taipei (Type A) personalities!" That would probably get a laugh, but perhaps at the cost of some audience trust.

People may smile and chuckle on cue at head humor, but inwardly they may feel we are trying to impress them, and they become resentful. Why turn people off or make them feel distrustful when we can tell a humorous personal story that includes everyone?

In the end, Laughter of the Head is usually stressful— even for those who are good at delivering it.

2. Laughter of the Spleen

Laughter of the Spleen is evoked by humor at the expense of a person or group. It may involve sexist, ageist, or racist put-downs, sexual innuendo, sarcasm, hostility, and barbs that pit people against one another. Most television sitcoms and stand-up comics seem to rely on Laughter of the Spleen.

Laughter of the Spleen makes most people uncomfortable, even when they don't show it, because nobody knows when the meanness will turn against *them*. Anybody could be the butt of the next joke. It tends to create an unhealthy atmosphere, especially at work. Sexual innuendo has taken the longest fall from grace, because it not only makes the workplace unproductive but can be cited in sexual harassment lawsuits.

In the workplace of the future, the old slap-on-the-back salesman with the raunchy jokes that put women down will no longer make it—at all, anywhere. But the person who can come in and tell a story, express a sentiment, convey a feeling, by their words or attitude, that reinforces a sense of community, is going to win. He or she will get the promotions, build longer-term relationships, earn a higher income, and get more satisfaction from the job.

3. Laughter of the Heart

Laughter of the Heart results from the humor of The Laughing Spirit. It recognizes in a lighthearted, good-natured way that we are all human, and that we all have great strengths and odd foibles. It bows to the human condition, and includes everybody. Laughter flows when we all share the embarrassment of the human experience.

Healthy humor observes the chatter of our minds, and reveals the hilarious secret that none of us has it all together, even though we all *pretend* to have it together. The humor of Bill Cosby, Lily Tomlin, and Garrison Keillor, and *The Full Monty,* my favorite movie of 1997, are examples of Laughter of the Heart. So are my early role models, Mike Nichols and Elaine May, who were funny because they told the truth about how men and women really interact with one another. All find their humor in the truth of human nature.

Laughter of the Heart is relaxing and good for office morale. It breaks tension, and makes everyone feel more whole and productive. It reinforces the feeling that we're all in this together, and hinges on high self-esteem.

Jokes and cleverness can easily and quickly turn into bad business. *Being human is funny enough,* and "non-toxic" heart humor opens up the audience to our message, be it information or inspiration.

Laughter Makes Us Whole

Why do we laugh? Researchers tell us that laughter is our natural way of releasing tension or conflict—even when we are not consciously aware of what that tension or conflict may be.

Humorist David Roche brings people together by sharing his own particular twist on universal conditions and fears. They laugh when he simply talks about what's going on with him, such as "what it's like to be in the male menopause with cold flashes, or God's cruel joke that as we all get older, women get more interested in sex and men get less interested—and there's only one three-week period when we're on the same page."

People feel safe because David talks about his own fears. "But they may have either those same fears or parallel fears. And normally people don't talk about this stuff," he says.

Donna Strickland is a nurse and humorist who conducts "Laughing Spirit Speaking Circles" at nursing homes all around the United States. She has a profound perspective on healthy humor:

> I see humor as having a "fluid spirit." Spontaneous humor just bubbles up. There is no road map for it. It requires that you let go of control. Show up, be present, tell the truth, and not try to control the outcome. You

flex and flow with your content, and with your audience. You have enough content, stories that let you go where the audience needs you to go—not just where *you* want to go. You are fluid and flexible—like water—which is the literal definition of humor.

Finding the Laughing Spirit

I coined the phrase "Laughing Spirit" when I was in Italy in 1980. My wife and I had just separated after a year of marriage, and it was the worst time of my life.

We had been writing comedy together for television, and she had suddenly stopped laughing at my jokes. I had lost my identity as a clever guy, a funny guy, and I was really miserable. I had to get out of the house, out of the relationship, and out of the country, so I decided to go to Europe.

For the first couple weeks there, I had a very bad attitude and a terrible time. I had lost my sense of humor, and nothing about Europe worked for me. But then one morning at seven o'clock, I was jolted awake when our train stopped at a little town just over the Italian border from France. I opened my eyes for another day of satisfying sulking, but what I saw outside the train window changed my perspective and brought me into The Laughing Spirit.

Two Italian trainmen in full uniform were having an animated conversation on the platform, waving their arms and gesturing wildly. I couldn't hear what they were saying, but it was obvious that they were living their lives passionately and humorously, in the spirit of full humanity, even at seven in the morning. As the train pulled away, I started letting their joy and vitality enter me, and suddenly I knew that something was going to change that day.

I was sharing a compartment with an Italian family of four. I didn't speak any Italian, and they didn't speak any English. I took out my traveler's phrase book, which until then I had used only to order food, and decided to have some fun. I turned to the list of common things you could say in Italian—things like hello, good-bye, excuse me—and I said, *"Mi scusi!"*

They all looked at me with great anticipation and said, *"Si, signore?"*

The next phrase was "Good morning," so I said in my best Brooklyn accent, *"Buon giorno!"*

They all said with great ebullience, *"Buon giorno, signore!!"*

The next entry that applied was "I don't speak Italian." *"Non parlo Italiano."* They laughed uproariously. Apparently, this was obvious. The next phrase was "I'm lost." I certainly was lost in my life, so I said, *"Non so dove mi trovo."*

They sighed, clutched their hands together, and said, *"Ohhh, signore!"* They felt my pain! I was connecting!

The next sentence was "Which way shall I go?" *"In quale direzione devo andare?"* And with that, all four of them pointed dramatically in the direction the train was going. Suddenly, I was laughing!

I laughed for the rest of the trip, in trains all over Europe, in four languages. I was still lost in my life, but I was connecting with people in the universal language of laughter that brings us together. I had finally met The Laughing Spirit, the common humanity that joins us all together in being lost.

When we connect with someone in this Laughing Spirit, we immediately get the heart connection—no matter what language we're speaking. It's not always about laughing; it's just a lighthearted connection that acknowledges that we're all lost, but we're together.

Forced Laughter

. . . .

The best humor is rarely planned. The old paradigm for humor is selling jokes; the new paradigm is *telling stories.*

Jokes can make an effective point when they are told skillfully and are particularly appropriate to the subject, but attempts to *make* a group laugh can backfire. Audiences tend to feel manipulated, resistant, distrustful, and even resentful when we ask them to laugh, pressure them to laugh, or feel embarrassed or disappointed if they don't laugh.

The contrived joke may get a laugh that's a "ha ha" from the head, but people often withhold the "ho ho's" from their hearts and the "hardy har har's" from their bellies.

When we tell a clever, snappy joke that doesn't really go anywhere, with the intention of just "loosening up the audience," we are actually creating distrust. People aren't sure where we're going; all they know is that we started off by trying to manipulate them into something.

Reaching "The Giddy Innards"

. . . .

To get the really good laugh, we want to be playful. We reach people's giddy innards by relaxing them with accounts of our own humanity, by letting them know that we are one with them, and by reliving our vulnerable moments, close calls, and poignant incidents involving career and family. They open up when we tell stories from our daily lives, and of our common foibles—true stories of heart and soul.

At a humor program I conducted for psychotherapists, a participant said, "I just can't seem to get to my humor, and I want to change that." When I had her address the group, she was deadly serious about being deadly serious. So I asked her just to talk to us about the stress of not being funny, and wanting to be funny. The pressure was off, and she started a natural riff that cracked everybody up.

We don't have to work for laughter; it is always abundantly available. In fact, we're *repressing natural laughter* all the time—and that pressure is released when we simply tell people in our own way, at a leisurely pace, about our real-life experiences, attitudes, limitations, personal paradoxes, or challenges.

Our own amusement at our predicament activates their natural laughter. When we tell the truth from the platform, without blame or shame, we automatically trigger corresponding stories in the audience members' lives. They remember that they are not alone and feel no resistance to laughing in communion with us. We've broken the tension of isolation—between us and them, and between the light and dark parts of all of us.

Of course, we need to get the hang of reliving our stories, rather than simply memorizing them, and of picking the right stories for the right occasion and connecting them to our topic or message. But this natural humor eventually works even for presenters who don't think they are funny and who have never had the knack for telling a joke well.

The rule of thumb is this: Never reach for a laugh or try to orchestrate a response. No laugh is worth risking credibility by appearing to manipulate the audience. Think of *"letting people laugh"* rather than "making people laugh." Humor always shows up when we respect and like our audience, and when we talk about things that genuinely amuse us. Our own amusement becomes infectious.

A Medical Report: "Grumpy Kills"

Dr. Bob Nozik is an ophthalmologist who speaks around the world to professional audiences of up to five thousand about the latest developments in eye surgery and disease treatment. With a reputation for eccentricity, he interjects humorous comments on the side when they come to mind. "This," he says, "gets the audience to listen more closely because they're never quite sure what I am going to say. It primes their minds, so it's good for learning. They sit there eagerly receptive, like sponges, ready to smile or to laugh."

It is a time-honored tradition for medical speakers to be boring, so during presentations at medical meetings there is usually a lot of conversation in the audience. Not when Dr. Nozik speaks.

There is a deeper importance to Bob's humor. When he talks about the factors that go into diagnosis, he says that the medical history provides 40 percent of the information, the physical examination provides 30 percent, the lab work 10 percent, consultation 10 percent, and intuition 10 percent. He says, "All great diagnosticians have learned to pay attention to their intuition."

For that intuition component, he says, doctors need to be more open to nonlinear types of thinking than they usually are. "Intuition is blocked by left-brain dominance," he says, "and part of my work with professional audiences is to open them up to areas they can't quantify. Humor is an opening into accessing that critical 10 percent, and this is how I bring laughter into the medical model. Doctors need to know that 'grumpy kills.' "

Bob helps the doctors access the right, intuitive side of

their brains, by connecting with them through their eyes. He becomes very aware of what's going on at any moment and of how everyone is seeing that moment. "While I'm talking," he says, "when I suddenly see something as funny, I give it voice. When someone catches a double meaning and reacts, even if I wasn't intending anything, I stop and enjoy their reaction."

This way, Bob connects with the whole audience on a basis of broader awareness. In the past he'd just move on through such "distractions," but now he picks up on them and smiles, makes a comment, acknowledges that there was a surprise moment of found humor. He'll plug into it and bring it up for everybody.

It makes the learning so much better when people are enjoying themselves. When they are primed to hear surprises and receive some sort of delight, they are more receptive to learning the crucial information they need to know. It doesn't take jokes, just a sense of connection related to a broadening of awareness of both speaker and listeners.

Dare to Be Boring

When I coached comedy, I always told people that who we are is funny enough, and they should just tell the truth and dare to be boring. Most comedians are addicted to laughter, so this was nearly impossible for them—but giving ourselves permission not to be funny opens up endless possibilities for humor.

Conventional speaking wisdom tells us that we should use humor to lighten people up, provide a change of pace, and relax the audience. But we can do all those things simply by being real and connecting. We can just stop and smile because somebody out there is sending us a friendly thought. That's a humor break, even if there is no laughter. It produces the same result—relieving tension. Connected speakers don't need humor, so they tend to draw laughs.

One speaker did a presentation for a civic group and several months later got a call to come emcee their awards presentation because they thought he was a humorist. "I hadn't meant my civic group talk to be particularly funny," he says. "I was just being natural and telling my own stories."

A business consultant says, "I always wanted to be funny. Now I don't have to worry about being funny. It comes out anyway when I am authentic." An educator reported on evaluations he received for his keynote talk at a national conference: "The feedback was that I was inspiring, stimulating, and funny. I was not trying to be funny, so I was."

All humor should be that natural. The Laughing Spirit is our natural state. The way to tap it is simply to be ourselves.

. . . .

Chapter 9

CREATING SUPPORT IN
YOUR TOUGHEST AUDIENCE:
TRUST IS CONTAGIOUS

You've done it all—learned to drop into the place where you are most authentic, practiced opening up, receiving, and connecting with your audience. You're reclaiming your Inner Speaker and making friends with stage fright.

"There's no such thing as an 'easy audience' for me. When I speak to even a few people, fear of saying the wrong thing and looking stupid just overwhelms me."

•

"My greatest fear is turning bright red if someone in the audience challenges me."

•

"To do a good job as a speaker I think I have to be intellectual, so I always feel that every audience is putting an enormous demand on me to get things right."

Then, *disaster strikes.* You find yourself in front of a nightmare group, in circumstances that even Mother Teresa would find challenging. It might be:

• The hemorrhaging crowd who have just learned their company is downsizing and they may well lose their jobs.

• The after-dinner crowd, sleepy

from too much food and drink, tired and cranky after a day of listening to speakers.

• The lunchtime crowd who have just been served their entrees as you are introduced, who are now wielding the noisiest knives and forks in creation while chatting with each other about the texture of the pasta or the baked chicken—and couldn't care less about the lonely figure in the front of the room.

• The crowd you never imagined, for whom you should never have been hired as a speaker—you are speaking on vegetarianism to spouses at a Texas cattlemen's convention, or to the New York Association of Bill Collectors on gentle telephone technique.

Disaster can also come in individually wrapped packages. One person—a drunk, a heckler, an unruly uninvited guest, a person who has to take over any room he is in—can present a challenge to even the most serene and centered speaker.

This chapter is about how to create support in any room. It is about tough audiences, speakers' nightmares, worst-case scenarios—and how to turn them all into wins.

Where Support Begins
. . . .

The truth is that most audiences are neutral, at worst. They are usually either indifferent or mildly interested, and a few start out enthusiastic. But when we're standing alone at the podium or the conference table, everybody can start looking like Attila the Hun. Sometimes our fears have some foundation—but we need to enter every room knowing that, regardless of what we find, we can create support for ourselves and our message.

Support begins with us. It's up to us to bring the support we've received in practicing transformational speaking into any room where we speak. The more we practice receiving, and the more we've come to *expect* support, the easier that becomes.

Richard and Antra Borofsky are Boston psychologists who specialize in relationships. What they say about one-to-one relationships applies to the speaker-audience relationship as well: "We usually think that to receive something, there has to be somebody who has something to give. But a skillful receiver can actually *create* what they want to receive. They can create the giving in the other person. Good receivers make good givers."

The truth is that, in any room, there are people who do want to support us. They may not be the first people we see, or the people on whom we first focus, but they are there. Somebody is biting into her chicken, thinking, "Oh, that must be tough on the person up there, to be speaking just as we start eating. I'll send a smile or give that person my attention." Another person remembers when he was in a similar difficult position in front of the room or in a meeting, and sends some goodwill.

We need to recognize these people, to seek out the pockets of support that exist in any room, and focus on them. We need to open up the electrical current between them and us—so that the *current* becomes the focal point and everyone else is irresistibly drawn into it.

One Friendly Face

Even in the most difficult rooms, there are usually one or two friendly faces. It's up to us to find those people, and speak directly to them. That one supportive connection becomes infectious. Before long, we've brought the whole audience along with us and created a network of good feelings. That connection is bound to be more interesting and more pleasant than anything else that's going on. When we receive the support that's available, other people get the idea—even when they don't look like they will.

A university professor who had spent decades in front of classrooms found a whole new level of connection by singling out the *one supportive person* in an audience: "The idea of taking a moment to receive the support that is naturally there, then connect with the one person who is most clearly supportive and start talking to that person, was a breakthrough for me. As an introvert, I'm at my best talking to one person at a time."

"I look for the one person with whom I feel safe," says a contractor and community leader. "Speak to that person, build the energy, and spread it from there. I can usually draw out at least one to three people. I'll see a glimmer in the eye or a nod of the head, and I'll stay with that person, let it grow to the person next to them and get some interaction going."

It is also true that you do yourself a disservice by jumping to a conclusion about how a person is reacting just based on what is displayed on their face. Some people simply don't register positive reactions on the surface, one or two may be having a bad day beyond anyone's control, and still others may be engrossed in your material to the point of being *dumbfounded*. In fact, almost every professional speaker I know has a story about an audience member who seemed to shoot an hour's worth of daggers or blanks at them and later came up to say that was the greatest speech they'd ever heard.

The Power of Trust

. . . .

When we walk to the front of the room, we can't ask ourselves, "Will these people support me, or not?" We need to know we are the *source* of that support, and that we can find that one friendly face. If we don't see it right away, we just hang in there until we do.

We don't wait to see if it's a "tough audience" or an "easy audience." We trust that we can allow *every* audience to become a supportive one.

Guaranteed supportive audiences, like those who gather to practice the principles of tranformational speaking, are a good place to develop this trust. Once we've experienced that level of support, over and over again, we come to expect it. And the greater our expectation of support, the easier it is to create support in a room that is not operating with instructions to support us. Through our expectation and trust, we actually train people to be there for us.

"When I open up, I'm inviting people to support me," says an advertising executive. "When the support comes, it invites me to open up even more. It just keeps getting better and better."

"Trouble" in the Audience:

The Graduate School of Public Speaking

. . . .

What if we have a heckler or drunk in the audience? Or someone who is better behaved than a heckler, but challenges us at every turn? Or people who sit sullenly, with their arms and legs crossed? Or people who walk out?

George was guest speaking at a community meeting on drug addiction when a man who seemed to be drunk began heckling him. Clever enough to zing him with a one-liner, poised and confident enough to prevail in a confrontation, George chose neither course. Rather, he stopped, walked toward the man, looked at him kindly, and asked, "Is something wrong?" And waited patiently as the room went silent. The man was speechless, and a person who *did* know what was wrong with him was at his side immediately.

As transformational speakers, we embrace the individual in any condition—crazy, hostile, wanting to leave—and treat him with dignity and respect. No matter how vicious or problematic the person becomes, we keep accepting and supporting him.

We model good behavior. We use the problem as part of our presentation. We treat the situation as an example of what we are saying. We embrace the opportunity to demonstrate our message, and so we don't get frightened of the person. We don't resist him or defend against him. We are open to him, hear him, and stay connected to him.

The rest of the room sees this, and gets behind us. When their energy aligns with ours, either the problem person will be swept back into the goodwill of the group, or he will leave. The audience and speaker work together like an immune system, finding one way or another to solve the problem. We're on the same side, working together for the good of the organism and all its parts.

Allowing for Magic

To deal with difficulties in an accepting, supportive way, we have to let go of our expectations about how the talk should go. We have to play the hand we're dealt, and make the best of it. The talk may turn out differently from what it would have been without that person in the audience, but we trust that it went the way it was supposed to go—and almost always it turns out to be better than it would have been without the trouble.

Instead of immediately reacting to trouble, pause to center yourself and to *include the audience in the solution.* An organizational consultant says, "If something goes wrong, I don't have to be the one to fix it, as I always tried to. This comes from recognizing the wisdom of the group. You can only pause when you don't believe that everything is going to hell in a hand basket and you're totally responsible and the only one who can save it."

Barbara Druker was giving a talk to a group of forty on "Creating Life Balance." There was a man off to one side in the front row who was somewhat rude and challenging in his demeanor. (Barbara later found out that he gave workshops on the same topic.) After a small group exercise, out of the corner of her eye, she thought she saw him raise his hand, so she turned to him and asked if his hand was up. He replied sarcastically, "No, I was picking my nose."

The audience laughed uneasily. Barbara centered herself, breathed deeply, and maintained total eye contact with him. "I was not at all reacting to the personality of the man I saw in front of me, not closing off to him, but staying open," she reports. "I opened energetically to connect with and receive his deeper self. I stayed focused like that for a few seconds, inviting him nonverbally to contribute."

He remained silent, so Barbara turned her focus back on the group, made eye contact with someone who looked supportive, and invited that person to report on her experience during the exercise. "I could feel the audience breathe a sigh of relief, that I was continuing my presentation unperturbed," she says.

As mentioned earlier it's like aikido. In this martial art, you don't fight or run from negative energy; you work *with* it and redirect it. Aikido experts believe that aggressive energy comes from a wounded place in the other person, and that it dissipates if you really connect with that person's true center.

A career counselor put it this way: "The way I speak to an audience that doesn't seem to be in agreement with me is to be in agreement with myself, in touch with myself, and the fact that I'm okay."

Chapter 10

SO YOU'RE GOING TO GIVE A TALK:
PREPARING FROM THE INSIDE OUT

> "Since childhood I wanted to speak out, but I always wondered: who am I?"
>
> •
>
> "I keep running into an inner voice saying 'you don't have anything of value to contribute; it's already been said and done.' "
>
> •
>
> "Rather than seeing me as nervous, people view me as not knowing my material, or being unprepared. I lose credibility."

Imagine that you've been practicing transformational speaking for a while. You've begun to find your Truth and your voice, and each week you're getting a stronger sense that you have a message to deliver.

You know this message would enhance people's lives, and you've even begun to envision spreading your wings and speaking about it in public. You don't know exactly how to get started, but you're about ready to do *something*.

Suddenly, out of the blue, your department head, church, or community group calls and asks you to give a presentation at their next meeting! What do you do?

This chapter covers the basics of getting ready for a talk—both internally, and on the podium.

It Starts with Your Attitude

. . . .

Speaking is one of the most powerful ways we can make a contribution, and we need to honor that in ourselves.

Adopt the attitude that you are a shining light, sent into the world to deliver this specific message. If people didn't need to hear it, you wouldn't be moved to share it.

You're not telling people "how it is" or shoving your point of view down their throats. You're simply sharing your own experience, giving them your unique perspective on a situation in which you've met a challenge, and offering it in the hope that they will find it as useful as you have.

I worked with Lency Spezzano, a healer in Hawaii, to find her message and develop her talk. Lency remembered being a very happy little girl who talked to birds and cats and flowers. When she was five, she tried to help her mother out of a depression by saying, "Mom, the world is an incredibly wonderful place. Life is just a miracle."

Her mother looked at her and said, "No, Lency, life is a struggle. You don't get to be happy till you die and go to heaven." With those words, Lency fell into a dark downward spiral of depression that lasted for many years. It took a long time and a lot of work to pull herself out of that spiral and see the light again. But today, Lency's talk is about moving from *darkness into light*. She is still in the tunnel sometimes, but she sees the light at its end and is a little ahead of other people. She shines her light for others so that they can keep moving.

This is all any of us can do. We can *shine the light of our own experience* on a situation, and hope that others are helped. We can't save them or make them act—but we can light the way.

When the talk becomes true and strong in itself, larger than you, and you become just the vehicle, the power of the truth takes over. You *become* what you're talking about, you are intimate with the audience because of your light, and in that truth and ultimate power, *you* become the service to the audience. Now they are connected to you, with you, and can experience your experience.

Knowing What to Say

Many of us know instinctively that we have something to say, but need to spend some time focusing in on exactly what our message is, and how best to deliver it.

Clients often tell me, "I know I have something to give, but I don't know how to frame it. I don't know how to put myself forward."

It's as if little Speaking Angels are sitting on their shoulders, nudging them to get out there even before they are 100 percent clear about what they want to say. Those angels are delivering the message: "It's time to get clear. If not now, when?"

The first thing I tell people is that we know more than we think we know about our message. It's just a matter of sitting down and figuring out what we do know.

Many people begin this process by picturing themselves standing behind a dark oak lectern in front of a large group of people—usually very judgmental, easily bored, critical people who have gathered to decide whether the speaker has any value as a purveyor of information or as a human being.

This is not a good place to start. Instead, sit down with a tablet of paper, and *ask yourself what you know about life*. You might do this with a trusted friend or coach. Here are some questions that might prompt ideas:

- What has life taught you?
- What have been the turning points in your life? In what

directions have you turned at these points? What have you learned?

· What secrets have you discovered?

· Who are the people who inspired you in your life?

· When you comfort or counsel friends, what do you usually wind up talking about?

· Into which areas of life do you have particularly clear insight?

· What are you good at?

· Where do you seem to have a unique perspective?

· What obstacles have you overcome? What did you use to overcome them?

Brick Walls That Become Teachers

Your message probably has something to do with obstacles, weaknesses, fears, failures, or *limitations that you have overcome.* You may have found a way through a problem that other people can use to get through similar problems, or through problems that are the same but not as extreme.

For instance, I know a businessman who has such severe dyslexia that he reads at a fourth-grade level, and yet he is extremely successful and very wealthy. He is in great demand as a speaker, and travels around the country talking about how to deal with learning disabilities.

People are inspired by his life, and how he overcame his limitation. He sees his dyslexia as a *gift.* Because it forced him to become a bigger person—and, in the end, it gave him his vehicle for expressing himself and serving people.

Our situations don't have to be as dramatic as the dyslexic businessman's. We find unique ways to overcome life's smaller difficulties every day.

Quite often, we *use our greatest strength to overcome our*

greatest limitation. We take something at which we are intu-itively brilliant, and apply it to our weakness. For example, my limitation was that I couldn't be heard. As the youngest in my family, I was never heard or given much credit—and this pattern carried over into my adult life. The backward, wounded part of me was nervousness, fear, and confusion about expressing myself. My great strength was that I had a deep, instinctive grasp of group dynamics. I could tell exactly what was going on in any group, without thinking about it.

As I started teaching and coaching, I began to apply my greatest strength to my greatest weakness. I experimented with using group support to encourage clearer, more con-nected communication and expression. As I did that, I saw that *my problem was a universal problem.*

A lot of people feel nervous and confused about express-ing themselves—and it turned out that group support was an almost universal solution. Speaking Circles, along with the principles of transformational speaking, are the result of us-ing my greatest strength to overcome my greatest obstacle.

When we use that chemistry, bringing the greatest strength and greatest weakness together to solve the prob-lem, then we have something to teach others. The next step is putting it out there. I could have packed up and said, "Well, *my* problem's solved. I'm going home." Letting people know about it, putting together a talk to promote it, and being will-ing to do circles for only a few people at first were the first steps in bringing transformational speaking out into the world.

We can also find our message by looking at turning points in our lives.

Turning Points

. . . .

Sometimes our message grows out of *turning points* that change the direction of our lives: a divorce, a marriage, the birth of a child, a death or illness, meeting a significant teacher, getting fired, moving to a new city, a career change, joining a spiritual group, getting a certain degree. Turning points are marked by crisis, opportunity, failure, and inspiration.

Often, these events determine what we do with our lives, and make us the people we are today. We can usually trace our passions and commitments back to them—or to the people involved in them. These formative experiences contain the roots of our passion, *and our message comes from our passion.*

We all know of people who found their message and their life's work in turning points. Candy Lightner founded MADD (Mothers Against Drunk Driving) after her child was killed by a drunk driver. Basketball's Magic Johnson began his work on behalf of people with HIV after he contracted the virus.

Sometimes we're reluctant to discuss these turning points in public because they seem too personal, or we don't trust our ability to share them well, or we're not sure what point to make, or we just don't seem to remember the right ones. *Telling the meaning of a turning point experience can take as little as a minute.* It can be very simple, and it is an extraordinarily effective tool—both for finding your message and for delivering it.

Big Small Moments

. . . .

Our messages can also come out of smaller, quieter moments. I once worked with the owner of a very successful employment agency who had been asked to give a talk and didn't know what to say. I asked her what was going on in her life and to describe a few incidents that had happened in the last few weeks.

She told the story of walking her daughter to her first day at kindergarten, and the little girl saying, "Mommy, you're squeezing my hand too tight!"

I asked her how that might apply to her business, and she suddenly realized that she had been squeezing her *managers* too tightly. Then I asked her what would happen if she went in and told her managers that story? She developed a professional talk called "Hands-Off Management" on promoting high self-esteem and self-direction among managers—letting go of the need to control and trusting managers to do a good job.

Another client was an antique specialist who wanted to start a speaking career. Her parents had been antique dealers and she'd known everything about this field since she was a child—but she couldn't quite find the particular slant, hook, or angle she wanted to use.

I knew what she did, but I kept asking her, "What do you do?" Each time, her answer got shorter. And each time, I asked her to tell me more succinctly what she did.

Finally, she said in frustration, "I feel like I was born in an antique shop!" That became the first sentence of her talk. It piqued people's interest and was the perfect lead for the kind of personal, intimate, cozy chat she liked to have with groups about antiques and the antique business.

Imagine Your Audience

Earlier I said that most people start by imagining a critical, easily bored audience—and many of them get so intimidated they never find their message. Instead, imagine yourself before a small, supportive group of people who really want to hear what you have to say.

What would be the first thing you'd say to this group? What do you want them to know about you? You may find your message there. If nothing comes to mind, just keep standing there, patient and relaxed. If you wait long enough for those first words, you'll probably have your lead sentence. If you just keep standing there in your imagination and coming up with things you want to tell them, you'll discover many of the elements of your talk.

Next, think about your through-line and title. *What is the one thing you want them to get?* What point of view do you want to impart to them? Your whole talk will be built around making sure this point gets delivered.

Then you can start thinking about your opening, and begin to structure your talk. We'll deal with the opening and structure in the next two chapters.

That's how you find your message and create your talk out of nothing.

You Have to Start Somewhere

You've found your message and used the next few chapters to prepare your talk. Now what? Where do you start?

Remember that community groups, professional associations, and service clubs are constantly open to speakers to "entertain the troops" for a half hour to an hour at no cost.

Do's and Don'ts

For your first talk, here are some basic reminders before you walk to the platform.

DO	DON'T
• Silently receive your listeners for at least one deep breath before you speak.	• Start talking immediately to cover up anxiety or project "confidence."
• Speak only to individuals, lingering with each person for three to five seconds before moving on.	• Speak to "the group" as a whole, darting or scanning your eyes to make surface eye contact with many.
• Speak in short sentences, pausing regularly to really connect with individuals.	• Connect your sentences with "and" or "so," and pull away from eye contact in transition between points.
• Leave longer silences between important points to let your words sink in and to give your listeners a chance to digest the information.	• Cover up natural silences with "um"s and "ah"s, rush to the next point to avoid "dead air," or switch your attention inward to prepare the next sentence.
• Stand relatively still and move slightly *toward* individuals as you speak to them.	• Pace from side to side to "cover the audience," while making staged gestures.
• Use relaxing humor based on your own experiences, if you use humor at all.	• Tell jokes, be clever, quick, glib, offhand, or cute.
• Stand there and receive your applause at the end of your talk, taking it into your heart.	• Walk off "modestly" as you are being applauded.

Local libraries and phone books have lists of these groups. Simply call the number, ask to speak to the program chairman, and tell him or her about your talk. Take advantage of speaking opportunities at your church, school, hospital, and neighborhood groups as well. The more practice you get, the better you become.

Many very successful speakers started out this way. As you gain experience and contacts, you can start charging money and speaking to larger groups.

If professional speaking interests you, look into joining a local chapter of the National Speakers Association. NSA has been my professional association since 1989, and its members typically are supportive and resourceful live wires. Call (602) 968–2552 for information.

And *don't be afraid to fail.* I bombed big time on my first professional speaking engagement. I'll never forget the look of pity on the faces of two hundred people at the San Francisco Airport Marriott Hotel as I lost my place several times and never really found it again. As I slunk off the stage to a tepid round of mercy applause, I never imagined I'd not only live to tell the tale, but that I'd become a professional speaker and speaking coach!

In the next two chapters, we'll start putting together the nuts and bolts of your actual talk.

. . . .

Chapter 11

THE PERFECT OPENING:

YOUR FIVE-MINUTE BLASTOFF

◎

When you first stand before a group, what you have in front of you is basically a disorganized collection of individuals. Most audiences are fragmented in two ways.

First, they aren't particularly connected with one another.

Second, each individual's attention is split in several different directions. They're thinking about a disagreement with a co-worker, their kid's report card, lunch, various doubts and fears, resentment over a conversation at dinner last night, sex, their financial situation, wouldn't it be better just to be lying on a beach in Tahiti, and a variety of other human concerns. These things are calling to them just as loudly as you are.

Most audience members are not consciously aware of these subtle dynamics. Nor do most speakers know that this is the game they are playing each time they step to the front of the room. But the truth is, you have five minutes to get your show on the road.

To grab your audience's attention, put them at ease, and

shape them into a community, you must first answer the four burning questions every audience has.

The four burning questions on every audience's mind are:

1. *Who are you?*

The personal, universal story answers this question by humanizing us, making us vulnerable, connecting them to us and to each other, showing them what makes us tick.

Remember to pause, receive their support, and make eye contact with one person before speaking your opening line: "Peoria, 1995. I was lying flat in a dentist's chair, bright lights shining in my eyes, people in surgical masks hovering above me . . ." Then pause again for a few seconds while the whole audience joins you in that time and place. Presto! You have created community.

2. *Why are you here?*

This is the logical conclusion to your personal story. What did you learn? What is the moral of the story? What about that story, when you follow the thread, brings you here today in all your passion to give them your message? "When I learned so tragically that no one need lose their teeth if they floss every day, I made it my life's work to get the word out."

3. *What are we going to do?*

Review your agenda for the talk in no more than three sentences. Tell them what you are going to tell them. "So today I will discuss the myths about plaque. I'll tell you about the truly scandalous nature of strep, and then I'll share the five secrets of flossing effectively."

4. What's in it for me?

Promise them a specific benefit. "By the time I'm done, you will see that flossing is fun and financially rewarding, and you'll never again leave home without it!"

With that flourish, pause to gather their agreement that they are in the right place and ready to come along with you. To do this, you can use phrases like:

- "Would this be useful to you?"
- "Are you in the right place?"
- "Any questions?"

It's easy to create your opening following this simple format.

Who Are You? Your Personal, Universal Story

On September 13, 1991, Mario Cuomo, then governor of New York and perennial noncandidate for president, stood before a restrained audience at the convention of the National Association of Broadcasters.

But as he told stories of his boyhood and his relationship with his mother, warm smiles spread through the room. Cuomo worked his magic in an easy, conversational way, with pauses to listen as his words sank into the broadcasters' hearts. At the end of his talk, he got a standing ovation—not by pumping up his audience, but by telling personal stories in a quiet conversational style.

The *San Francisco Chronicle* ended its report on the event with "Although the broadcasters initially appeared to be cool to Cuomo, they warmed to him as he told stories of his youth and of his mother, who speaks to him in Italian."

Mario Cuomo warmed up a cold audience with a personal

story that had universal applications. Every broadcaster in the room had some warm childhood memories, and they were triggered as Cuomo relived his. Like Cuomo, we can connect with our audience by sharing stories that are real and unique to us, but also so universal that everyone has his or her own version of them and feels immediate empathy with us.

The personal, universal story—related in a conversational, emotionally open style in three minutes or less—makes us one with our audience. It compels rapt attention by breaking the illusion of separation and bonding us as a group. We are all grounded in our common humanity. While we are telling our story, the audience members are finding their own similar stories. They know that we are as vulnerable as they are, and that we are here as one of them.

We can approach an individual by simply looking into his or her eyes and saying, "Hello." But to bond a group of people to us, and to one another, we have to tell a story to which everyone can relate. We let everyone sit back, remembering a similar emotional experience. In this way, we form the group into a community.

I believe that there is a perfect opening for every audience. Recently I spoke to the American Association of Medical Transcriptionists and got their attention with this opening:

> In 1970 I was diagnosed with testicular melanoma, and had a transperitonial lymph node dissection.
>
> I'm telling you this for two reasons. One, this is the first audience I've ever spoken to who would understand just what that means. [Laughter] And secondly, when I researched what you folks do, I realized that there must have been a medical transcriptionist involved in my successful treatment, but that the nature

of this work keeps you in the background. So this is the first chance I've had to say . . . thank you.

When I left a long pause for my gratitude to sink in, a chorus spontaneously answered, "You're welcome!"

"Now," I said after another pause, "what can I do for *you?*" We were completely connected, and that opening started a wonderful day.

We may deliver our personal, universal story in a casual, conversational style—but we remember that it has a job to do. It has to put our audience at ease with us, and with one another. It has to bring us all together into a community.

Our opening story is the focal point of a perfect opening. It answers the first question on the audience's mind: "Who are you?"

Seven Steps to the Perfect Opening
. . . .

Here is another way to look at presenting the perfect opening. It includes steps for connecting with your audience, as well as for telling your personal, universal story and answering the four burning questions. But even before Step One there is an attitude to take toward your audience that will allow the other steps to flow. I'll call it Step Zero.

Step Zero. Before you step onto the podium.

While you are being introduced, stand in front of the room near your introducer and appreciate the audience. Start this step *anytime* before the talk. During the hour prior to your introduction, for instance, don't isolate yourself to go over your lines. If the group is doing other business, or eating a meal, sit among them and *be* with them. Get in touch with your heart connection to them.

Remember that *they want you to do well.* Focus on them

instead of on yourself. Think about what they do in their work lives and put yourself in their shoes. Résumé expert Yana Parker says, "Getting out of me and into them transforms my experience. They need something and I've got it. How absurd it was to be afraid of audiences. They're afraid to speak like that themselves. They are awestruck that anyone can get up and talk in front of that many people."

Now we are ready for the seven steps:

Step 1. Your nonverbal opening.

When the applause ends, we have a tendency to start talking immediately. Instead, honor the silence for at least five to ten seconds. Center yourself and breathe. You may want to close your eyes for a moment or gently flex your knees. Take in the entire room, then individual faces. Feel the goodwill for you out there. The foundation of our authentically supportive relationship with the audience is laid *before we say a word*. Resist the urge to send out an ingratiating smile that begs, "Please like me." Don't speak until you make true eye contact with one individual beaming at you. Say your first sentence directly to that person.

This nonverbal opening is so critical for preparing yourself and your listeners for your opening story, I want to share with you an interesting case history.

I was in the home of Alice Waters, world-famous chef and owner of Chez Panisse in Berkeley, California. This passionate advocate for sustainable agriculture was standing in her kitchen telling me about the fear she faces when she first stands up in front of the large and distinguished audiences she is asked to share her ideas with. In the coming week she would be presenting a talk to a group of dignitaries that would include Vice President Al Gore.

I asked Alice to identify the key element that made her

so successful in her field. She responded that she has a wonderful relationship with food.

Looking around her well-appointed, cozy kitchen, I asked, "Alice, when you make a salad, do you just throw the lettuce on this chopping board and start cutting it up?" She looked horrified and shook her head. I said, "I'll bet you place it gently on the board and honor it with respect and love before you cut into it." Yes, she nodded.

"Alice, I don't have that kind of relationship with food. I just throw the lettuce down and cut it up," I confessed. She frowned and I went on, telling her about my blind spot around food, just like the one she had with audiences. I suggested that before saying a word at her upcoming talk, she look at the faceless mass of the audience as she would regard a roomful of heads of lettuce. Maybe even spot a couple of tomatoes in the crowd. Take at least fifteen seconds of silence to honor those fresh faces, appreciate their beauty, and breathe with them. *Then* speak to them.

A week later, Alice called to say, "It worked! That was the best speech I've ever given." She had appreciated the audience silently and reverently before diving into them!

Can your approach to an audience make or break a talk in the first fifteen seconds? Absolutely.

The conventional wisdom in public speaking has always been to "open with confidence," but for those of us not blessed with nerves of steel and tongues of silver, opening with confidence in the most stressful situation known to humans is out of the question. The only alternative seems to be to fake it.

But here's a whole new option: approach the podium not with a show of confidence, but with genuine *receptivity*. It's easier—once you get the hang of it—and far more effective than any performance technique. It's actually the *absence* of technique. When you stop to notice your audience and *really* let them in before speaking to them, you are honoring a relationship, not perfecting a technique.

When Alice Waters honors her lettuce before chopping it up, she is not practicing a culinary technique. By honoring her audience in a similar way, she is bringing some of the natural confidence she has in the kitchen into the realm of public speaking, where she *doesn't* have natural confidence.

What do you have a special relationship with—like the one Alice has with fresh vegetables—that you can invite those faceless masses into before you say a word? If you love to arrange flowers, you might see the audience as a colorful garden of lovely blossoms, and breathe in their fragrance. Are you a connoisseur of interesting hair? Nice clothes? Beautiful faces? Enjoy them with soft, receptive eyes; this is not about staring.

Perhaps you are a person who takes seriously the metaphor, "the eyes are windows to the soul." Well, then, take the time to look through some windows, and let those souls look back through yours.

The most direct course for those of us who like people (at least one-on-one) is to simply appreciate some of them, *one at a time,* as you let them look at *you.*

Eventually, any device that helps you get there, whether it's seeing your audience as heads of lettuce, hearts of artichoke, or souls of sweetness, will dissolve when you get comfortable opening every talk with just you and them and the silence. After experiencing the relaxation of opening in silent appreciation a few times, Alice Waters no longer needs to turn her audience into a salad.

Step 2. *Your opening line.*

Resist the temptation to open with a nicety, such as, "It's great to be here," or "Thank you, Maureen, for that wonderful introduction." Instead, thank your introducer personally as he or she leaves the stage and concentrate on the audience once you arrive at the podium.

Unless you are an accomplished humorist, it's rarely a good idea to open with a joke. The rewards are minimal and the risks are great.

Your opening line should bring listeners right into your personal, universal story. Make it short, and make it something that transports them directly to a specific time, place, and situation. Some examples:

- "Kansas City, Missouri. 1980. I got fired."
- "When I graduated from college, I knew everything."
- "Got a call from my mom last night." (Only if you really did get that call.)

When everybody travels with you to that point in time and space, you all have a common meeting ground and become a community. Pause to let them gather around you.

Step 3.   The rest of your personal, universal story.

Don't just recite it, but don't force feelings on the audience by overdramatizing it. Tell the story clearly and with some emotional content, but let the audience have *their own* feelings. Relive this turning point in your life. It might involve a failure or limitation, an obstacle in your path, perhaps an episode featuring a person who influenced your life. The rest of your story should take no more than three minutes. You may expand on the story in the body of your talk, but here in the opening, you are giving the headline version.

Step 4.   Transition to the present.

In three to five sentences, connect that story, and what you learned from it, to *why you are here today* to talk with them about your topic. In the course of this transition, make sure to honor your audience for what they had to accomplish already to be here.

Step 5. Brief agenda.

Outline the major points you will cover in three or four concise headline sentences.

Step 6. Your promise.

In one sentence, make the most provocative promise you can comfortably guarantee. This is your contract with them, and you intend to deliver on it. I worked with one woman whose promise is, "And when I am done today, you will know exactly how to reverse the aging process." And she delivers! End this sentence with a flourish, if this is comfortable for you—as if you were ending a talk.

Step 7. Collecting agreement.

At this point, you will probably be facing a sea of faces nodding, "Yes, yes, yes. We are with you!" In silence, survey the audience to collect their agreement that they are in the right room and ready to take off with you. Some speakers verbalize this step with phrases like, "Okay?" "Are you ready?" "Will this be helpful?"

This is the end of the beginning. Your opening is actually a minitalk, separate from the body of your talk. Gathering the agreement of your audience gives it closure, and signals that you are moving on to the talk itself.

The "Rapt Attention" Opening

Let's look at how these principles might work in an actual opening. Since this book is about transformational speaking, I'll give you an opening that I might use to introduce this work to an audience of professional speakers. The name of this talk is "How to Compel Rapt Attention Every Time You Speak," and here is my opening:

> One of my first public presentations was at a Veterans Administration hospital respite program for primary caregivers. The audience was mostly wives of disabled veterans. I came on after two nurses who demonstrated how to move a patient from bed to wheelchair. Serious business. Suddenly I was being introduced to talk about . . . *humor.*
>
> As I stepped to the platform on buckling knees, I felt anything but funny. Gazing out at a sea of faces that looked like they hadn't cracked a smile in years, I thought, "What can I possibly tell these women about humor?"
>
> Instead of launching into my talk, I stammered, in hopeful desperation, "Have any of you used humor to cope with your situation?" A seventy-year-old woman raised her hand and saved my life. She said, "My husband and I have always laughed a lot, and we still do. He has Alzheimer's disease and every morning he sort of forgets who I am and proposes marriage. I love it! We laugh and laugh."
>
> One by one the women shared their tragic *and* comic experiences, which clearly made the point that it was *laughter* that kept them going. They turned out to be the most cheerful, uplifting audience I've ever had.

I have told a personal, universal story that opens a window on my world and answers Question No. 1: "Who are you?"

I would continue:

> What I learned from that experience was that any audience is potentially funnier than any speaker. In fact,

every audience is a treasure trove of experience and wisdom that no speaker can match, and that resource will surface to the extent that the speaker puts a priority on *relationship* with that audience, ahead of the material.

As professional speakers, you are in a unique position to bring out the best in people. I'm here today to show you how to bring out the best in every group you face, so that they will bring out the best in you—whether you are doing an interactive program or a straight talk.

This answers Question No. 2: "Why are you here?"
I would continue:

I will first discuss the true nature of the speaker-audience relationship, and how it has been misunderstood. I will show you how to use this new understanding to open every talk in natural rapport that compels rapt attention from the first moment to the last.

Then I will provide you with a set of lifetime tools for developing audience rapport in your own natural style. You will understand why I say "There's no technique like no technique."

We now know the answer to Question No. 3: "What are we going to do?"
"When our time together today is over," my opening concluded, "you will understand exactly what it takes for you to be irresistible to audiences—without putting on a performance."

This answers Question No. 4: "What's in it for me?"

Letting Them Know You Care

. . . .

Internet marketing guru Dan Janal speaks at sixty to seventy conferences a year and is a convert to the vulnerable opening. He says, "I used to open like 99 percent of technical speakers do: perfunctorily with an overview of the agenda. I thought audiences wanted a brain dump of everything I know about a subject."

But Dan has learned that the old saw is true: "They don't care what you know until they know that you care." By opening with a true story that humanizes him and ties in with the technical topic he's there to talk about, he finds that he's far more effective. The bottom line is that because he makes the topic personal, conference attendees are more open to him, learn more, and give better evaluations. "They feel they know me and are more willing to buy my services and my books—and to recommend me to others," he says.

Dan feels the audience rooting for him to emerge victorious in the stories he likes to tell, so that when he's ready to begin the nuts and bolts of the presentation they're already won over to his side. With people paying good money to hear the infallible expert, he never thought that such vulnerability would work, but he's learned that it's okay to expose mistakes as long as he can express what he learned from them.

He says, "People love jumping on the roller-coaster where you build up to something and you fail and then you pick yourself up and go on to even greater heights." They can see themselves in those stories, and they can make their own adjustments to relate the speaker's experience to theirs.

What a wonderful message to carry up to the podium, that you don't have to be Superman to be successful, that you can make mistakes and still be effective!

Michael Killen, a business consultant in advanced technology, also learned the benefits of opening a technical talk with vulnerability. He recently spoke in London to one hundred multinational executives on "The Future of Phone Cards." In his opening he talked about being a D student in high school and failing to go to college. After the talk, a colleague admonished him: "Don't ever tell that story in public again! It diminishes the respect the world has for Killen & Associates." Immediately after he said that, Michael reports, "three people came up to me, from Singapore, Germany, and Hungary, each wanting to know about the storytelling technique I used that touched their hearts. I can trace over $100,000 in business to that talk."

The Thin Line Between Vulnerability and Therapy
. . . .

John Caple, business consultant and author of *The Ultimate Interview* (Doubleday), sees himself as a highly controlled person who hadn't thought it appropriate to get teary-eyed in front of a corporate audience, especially since most of his business comes from his public speaking about leadership development. But when he told an emotional story about a friend of his, the results were so dramatic that he has since told it dozens of times.

As he relates it, "Bob was a Harvard Business School classmate, and our wives and families became friends. He was hugely successful in Silicon Valley, was Entrepreneur of the Year, and died at age forty-nine of lung cancer because he stopped smoking too late."

The point John makes with this story is that no matter how successful and brilliant you are, if you don't live a balanced life, you end up a loser. Bob didn't realize how soon the chips would be called in. John says, "His wife confided in me how much he was missed even before he died, and how much *he* missed by working so much and spending so little time with the children."

The story reached his audiences and raised the quality of his talks, and in letting himself go through the feelings of sadness and loss about his friend so many times, John worked through his own grief about it. In fact, he noticed that he stopped telling that story, "probably because it is no longer so charged for me," he guesses.

John's experience brings up two important points. One, even the best opening story has a finite shelf life. It only works when the story is still charged for the speaker. We must constantly bring in new stories that reflect what is meaningful for us now. That explains why some speakers who depend on the same signature story year in and year out come off flat. And sometimes telling the same story over and over in the same way, because their livelihood seems to depend on it, keeps them from growing past that story.

Point two—in storytelling there is a fine line between self-indulgence and vulnerability. John obviously got therapeutic value from publicly working through the grief of his friend's story. I concur with John's assessment of the distinction: "To me, it relates to getting clear about intent. My intent is to serve the audience. I believe that the second half of life is about service, and when you are clear on that, you do whatever it takes."

The purpose of public speaking is not to do therapy on oneself, though therapeutic value can be a happy by-product.

Opening with the Obvious
. . . .

If there is something about you that the audience can't help but notice, you need to answer their concerns immediately.

When David Roche gets up to speak about diversity, it is apparent that he has a severe facial disfigurement. He opens:

> I was born with this face. For most of my life I have felt deeply ashamed of it. Now I recognize it as an elaborately disguised gift from God. Oh, not a gift I was ecstatic about receiving. Did I say, "Oh! That's exquisite! How did you know what I wanted, God?" No . . . it was, "Oh, God! You shouldn't have! You really shouldn't have!" But my face *is* a gift, because my shadow side is on the outside where I have had to deal with it.

Brief Openings
. . . .

An opening story should be no more than about three minutes, but there is no limit on how brief it can be. The shortest effective one I ever heard was by a woman on the topic of relationships. Her opening "story," said with exasperation, was: "Men!!!" followed by a long pause. That said it all.

Peter Mayfield, founder of CityRock, Inc., corporate training program in wilderness learning experiences, used to say the usual: "Thanks, I'm glad to be here."

Now he takes the time to tune in to his audience before he says, "I climb mountains." After a long pause he adds, "I climb all types of mountains. [Another pause.] Short rocks on the beach. Tall snowy peaks."

Those three opening words resonate with his being. "This is what I do," he says, "and the clarity and directness sets a tone."

Taking the time to look at the audience and take in the room, then saying those words, catches their interest and brings them into the moment. They pay rapt attention to the rest of the talk.

Opening a Sharing Circle
. . . .

In some situations, such as an ongoing support group, opening with group participation rather than a story by the leader may be appropriate. In these cases, it's often a good idea to allow the *group,* rather than the facilitator, to determine the agenda for the discussion.

One counselor used to open his men's groups for recovering drug addicts by asking them to respond to a question, such as, "What have you been proud of about yourself the past week?" Now, instead, he asks each of them to share whatever they want to, and then he makes up a question based on a theme that usually emerges.

"By doing this," he says, "we come up with a question that is much more relevant and timely. It gets them right to where they are." It lets *them* make the agenda and draw their own lessons from the sharing that happens, rather than him coming up with something that may be a diversion from a real concern of theirs.

Breaking the Rules
. . . .

Like any other art, when you master the fundamentals, you can play with the form, color outside the lines. When you master relationship with audience you may find yourself giving up these guidelines for "The Perfect Opening," and letting the relationship dictate the flow. To what extent you can do this depends in part on the nature of the speaking engagement.

For instance, Dr. Elayne Savage, in her book tour to promote *Don't Take It Personally! The Art of Dealing With Rejection* (New Harbinger), stopped planning her speeches. She says that every talk is different, and when she stands up and looks into eyes and hearts, she is available to those who are open and willing to connect with her. "When I experience acceptance I relax and engage in that wonderful reciprocal energy," she says. "There's nothing like it."

Melody Ermachild Chavis speaks about her work as a private investigator in death row cases and as a community activist. Her practice now when she's about to make a speech is to sit with herself, and search her heart and her mind for a fresh insight, or for what is bothering her.

She says, "I relax into that insight and just meet the audience and immediately start by saying it, without preliminaries." For instance, she might say, "What's really breaking my heart right now is that . . ." Opening with an immediate concern, rather than having a prepared paragraph about a topic, is what works for her.

Blasting Off

Opening a talk is a little like launching a spacecraft. Before you can take off, you need to go around in your van and pick people up where they live, gather them on the launching pad, invite them into the rocket, show them to their seats, and buckle them in.

That's what you do with your five-minute opening. You connect them with you and with one another through your personal, universal story. You answer with crystal clarity the four questions on everybody's mind. You get their agreement that they want what you're offering, and you create community and empathy. Now you're ready to blast off!

In the next chapter, we answer the question, "What next?"

. . . .

Chapter 12

HOW TO STRUCTURE A TRULY

TRANSFORMATIONAL TALK

◎

This chapter is about structuring your talk so that it reaches the most people, in the most powerful way. The structure isn't meant to limit or stifle your creativity, but to make it easier for you to communicate, and easier for the audience to hear you.

Four-Part Harmony: The Basic Parts of a Successful Talk
. . . .

Well-structured talks often have four parts.

You already know about one of them, the opening. In those first five minutes, you ground and connect the audience by reliving a concise version of your personal, universal story and answering the four burning questions: Who are you? Why are you here? What are we going to do? What's in it for me? Then you're ready for blastoff, but where do you go next?

You blast off the way every shuttle mission does—into a beautiful *arc* against the clear blue sky. The next three parts of your talk are the ARC elements—*Awareness, Reframing, and Commitment to Action.*

Awareness defines the problem or issue.

You give some brief historical background, and tell stories about how you or others first encountered the difficulty. Mention ways the problem might affect your audience's lives. Trigger their connections with the issue. What exactly is *wrong?* Why is it *important* to them? Make sure everyone is on the same page and has a personal connection with the problem.

Reframing describes a new paradigm, and shows how you learned to look at the situation from a whole new angle, as an opportunity for growth or better business.

This is the meat and magic of the talk, where you turn the *problem* into a *possibility.* Use logic and personal stories to turn the audience's way of approaching this problem upside down.

Commitment to Action.

What steps can your audience take *now* to get the desired result?

With *Awareness,* you grab their thinking.

With *Reframing,* you turn their thinking around.

With *Commitment to Action,* you catapult their thinking into the future.

At some point, you may choose to move away from this structure—but my advice is to *master it before you let it go.* Let's look at each of these three ARC elements.

Awareness of the Problem

In the Awareness part of your talk, you describe clearly what the problem is *for your audience,* and lay out some of the current barriers to success in this area.

If you were talking about "What Individuals Can Do for the Environment," for instance, you might mention the rape of the rain forests, oil spills, and other global situations—but you might also show how their own health and well-being are affected, and tell some moving stories about individuals in similar circumstances who have suffered.

You might talk about why current political efforts on behalf of the environment have not succeeded: big corporate lobbyists blocking effective legislation, the lack of cooperation among nations, denial and apathy on the part of individuals, and Third World countries willing to "slash and burn" for quick profits, to name a few. You might describe how, in the face of these massive problems, and powerful barriers to solutions, most individuals throw up their hands. They don't believe they can do anything worthwhile on behalf of the environment—and so nothing gets done. Nobody fights the bad guys.

If you were talking about how to have more self-esteem, you might make clear exactly what you meant by self-esteem and then describe how elusive it seems for many of us. Even when we do everything right—great relationship, lots of money, a fabulous house or car—lack of self-esteem seems to be a chronic and pervasive problem in our society. You would illustrate your points with personal stories, and stories about others, until everyone recognized exactly what doesn't work about the present situation.

Some questions to ask yourself in putting together the Awareness part of your talk are:

- What is the problem about which you are passionate?
- Why does the problem exist?
- What efforts have been tried to fix it?
- Why have these efforts failed, or met with only limited success?

Once we know what the problem is, we can begin to turn it around.

Reframing: A New Paradigm That Solves the Problem
. . . .

Reframing is the magic trick within your talk. You pinpoint the false assumptions that keep people from succeeding in your area of expertise. You bust the old paradigm, or way of thinking, and show through your own experience that *a solution lies in looking at the problem in a new way—your way.*

You might share with the audience how you had your back to the wall—and then miraculously, you saw a new way of looking at the situation. When you *turned your thinking around* and discarded the old assumptions, you started to get results.

You shatter the conventional wisdom on your subject, and bring in the element of surprise. Your listeners think, "Aha!" You take the problem and spin it into an opportunity. This is your punch line, your twist, the alchemy you used to turn disaster into advantage.

Your audience may already suspect that the conventional wisdom is way off the mark. *They wouldn't have come to your program if they had the solution.* They will follow you anywhere if you systematically challenge what "those who know" are saying and give them new ways to see and solve the problem.

Show them how you came to your new paradigm. Perhaps you had just spearheaded a campaign for environmental legislation—and taken a beating. There you were, depressed at home watching the discouraging results come in on the evening news, and the very next story, after the stunning defeat of your campaign, was about an elderly lady who collected recyclable items from the park every afternoon and felt utterly fulfilled in making her contribution to the environment.

She had never even heard of your proposition, but she talked to the reporter about how good she felt about herself and what she was doing, and her smile lit up the screen.

Maybe you realized that, for you, the answer was moving your environmental campaign into your home, and onto a smaller scale where *you* were in charge of whether you won or lost. You set up your own recycling program, educated yourself and your kids about product pollution, started "buying green," and did everything you could around the house to support the environment.

You started feeling terrific about your efforts and realized that if *everybody* did the same thing, the environment would be helped exponentially. Not only that, but everyone would feel more effective, happier, and more in control.

The paradigm shift is from thinking about the environment politically to thinking about it *personally,* from thinking globally to thinking *locally.*

For the talk on self-esteem, perhaps you experienced a crashing depression when you got everything you thought would make you happy and give you high self-esteem—and then realized that you still didn't like yourself very much. That crash was the incentive to explore what did give you self-esteem and make you happy, and you discovered that self-esteem comes from *within,* not from the external things by which society tends to define it. You explored several good ways to nurture self-esteem from within, and found that they worked! Again, you approached the problem from a whole new angle, and applied a new paradigm.

Show through *your* success and enthusiasm that if your audience gives up the old ideas and concepts about how to handle the problem, *they* can have the same success.

Once the new paradigm has sunk in, and they've had their epiphany, you can help them make the commitment to action.

Commitment to Action
. . . .

If you've gotten your audience on the edge of their seats with
a great opening, defined the situation clearly, and offered an
exciting new way of looking at it, they'll be eager to know
what they can do right away. Make sure you have something to
tell them. Bring to your talk a list of *specific action steps* they
can take to solve the problem in their own lives.

You might offer five or ten things they can do around their
homes to protect the environment, or things they can do to
nurture self-esteem from within. These are the tools they can
use right away to get unstuck and begin solving the problem.
End with the simplest, easiest, most inviting step they can
take—or ask if *they* want to share any steps they've committed to taking right away.

Finally, wrap up your talk with an inspirational quote, or
perhaps a closing piece from your opening story, or by taking
a minute to tell them what it has been like for you to spend
this time with them. Tell them your hopes for them, and invite them to contact you if there is anything you can do to
support them.

Just as your opening is really a "closing"—to sell them on
listening to you—your closing is an opening to their relationship with your solutions *and a lifetime relationship with you.*

Putting It All Together
. . . .

Now it's time to sit down to structure your talk. You've been
honing your point of view for years, and living your message.
To bring home your point, you have at your disposal hundreds
of analogies, metaphors, anecdotes, facts, observations, and
quotes—more than you could ever use.

But at any given moment, sitting in front of a blank piece of paper, it may be hard to remember any of them. Or you may remember *all* of them, and have no idea which to use and which to toss.

Here is a method I use to let the talk emerge naturally, organically, and at its own pace. Choose three walls of your office, or get three huge pieces of posterboard. Or start three special computer files. Designate one wall or posterboard or file as PART ONE: AWARENESS. Designate another as PART TWO: REFRAMING, and a third as PART THREE: COMMITMENT TO ACTION.

Next, get stacks of sticky notes, large and small. Let your ideas, stories, and thoughts rise naturally out of your mind, in no particular order. Whenever something occurs to you that you might want to include in your talk, jot it down on a sticky note, and stick it up on the appropriate wall or posterboard, or type it into the appropriate computer file.

Is it part of *defining* the basic problem? Is it part of the *paradigm shift?* Is it part of a *program of action?* Stick it there and then let it go. *Daydream, brainstorm, remember,* and *reflect.* Over a period of hours, days, a week, you can literally empty your life into your talk! It's a natural way of organizing and letting your talk emerge easily out of your consciousness.

Next, take each of the three parts and make a minitalk out of it. Start each part with a "hello story" that illustrates the point you are about to make. Don't begin with "Okay, let's define the problem." Rather, open the body of your talk with a brief story that lends itself to a definition of the problem. At the end of Part One, *tell them* that you have defined the problem.

Open Part Two with another brief story, this one illustrating dramatic success with a new paradigm, and spell out the meaning of what you have just told them. Then launch into Part Two. End Part Two with enthusiasm, summarizing the new paradigm, and then after a deliberate hush, tell a story that brings your listeners into the realm of taking action.

The "Rapt Attention" Talk

In the last chapter, I gave you the opening for my hypothetical talk on "How to Compel Rapt Attention Every Time You Speak." Here is how it fits with the rest of the talk.

The "Rapt Attention" Opening

The personal, universal story I used was about speaking on laughter to women in a VA class on how to care for their disabled husbands—and realizing that they knew more than I could ever hope to learn about using humor to cope with difficult situations.

The larger application was that any audience is potentially funnier and wiser than any speaker. I expanded on that to say that every audience is a treasure trove of experience and wisdom that no speaker can match—and suggested that the way to tap this treasure is to put a priority on the *relationship* with the audience.

I promised that I would show them how to bring out the best in every group, and give them tools for building natural rapport and relationship with the audience to compel rapt attention from the first moment to the last.

After I collected their agreement that this was something they wanted, I moved into the body of the talk—taking on the ARC elements one by one.

"Rapt Attention" Part One: Awareness

I define the problem by talking about how the relationship between speaker and audience has been traditionally misunderstood, leading to an epidemic of stage fright in our society. To lead into that discussion, I open with a question and a personal story about my own stage fright.

"I became a public speaking coach because I had the world's worst stage fright. Who here has stage fright?" [I raise my hand to indicate that's what I'm asking them to do. Most of them raise their hands.] "And the rest of you are too frightened to raise your hands?" [Laughter]

"The first talk I ever gave was a disaster." Here I tell the story of my bar mitzvah speech that I related in chapter 1, and everyone roared when I recited the traditional words—"Today I am a man"—in a squeaky soprano. The story ends with the idea that radiating "vibrant vulnerability" is the key to building audience rapport.

Through stories and by asking the audience to recall speakers they've heard, I identify the problem: most speakers work so hard to project confidence and power that they sacrifice a genuine, vulnerable relationship with the audience. Or they are so focused on their content that they forget about connection. I also talk about how aspiring speakers see this unnatural approach modeled so often that they assume it is the path to successful speaking and struggle blindly upstream, without much notion of connection. People with stage fright are especially at risk here, since the confident, impervious "presence" they think they must assume in front of a group is so far from what they actually feel.

Finally, after exploring what goes awry in public speaking, I conclude that the basic problem is the unexamined nature of the speaker-audience relationship. Then I pause for as much as fifteen seconds as we all ponder the problem and its implications.

If this were a two-hour workshop, I would invite individuals to share their experience of speaking in public. If it were a half-day or full-day workshop, I would divide the audience into smaller groups of four to share experiences, then have a few people share with the entire group.

This is the end of Part One.

"Rapt Attention" Part Two: Reframing

Part Two starts with the good news that there is another way, an entirely new paradigm for connecting with an audience.

I illustrate with stories the difference between being dynamic (like some of the great speakers with whom we might compare ourselves: Winston Churchill, Franklin D. Roosevelt, Martin Luther King) and being magnetic, which is something *we can all do* by being willing to receive the audience's support. I talk about listening, connection, vibrant vulnerability, and the true nature of the speaker-audience relationship.

By the end of Part Two, I have made the point that being real, and being in connection with our audience, lets us communicate in deeper, more effective, and more life-enhancing ways, and that performance anxiety can be transformed into a *strength* when we give up masking it.

Now that we have defined the problem and reframed it, we can move on to Part Three, Commitment to Action.

"Rapt Attention" Part Three: Commitment to Action

Part Three gives people action steps to take these insights out into the world.

First, I talk about nurturing transformational speaking attitudes in Speaking Circles—and how once they have experienced the immediate and compelling benefits of a Circle, they will have lifelong tools for developing instant and natural audience rapport.

At this point, we divide into groups of four and have fifteen-minute mini-Speaking Circles so that they get a taste of the experience and become inspired to go out and form their own Circles. First, they go around the circle once for each person to receive thirty seconds of silent support. Then group members get two minutes apiece to talk about whatever is on their minds while receiving positive attention from the group.

Depending on how much time is available, a few people may use the whole room as their Speaking Circle, and share their insights or reactions to the concept with everyone. I try to have at least one person with severe stage fright come to the front of the room to demonstrate a "miracle healing."

Then I tell them how to start their own Speaking Circles at home or at work, and provide handouts describing the guidelines. (This information is in chapter 13.)

Early in my speaking career, I closed my talks with an inspiring story, quote, or poem. But I've discovered that what works better for me is not a neat ending, but a closing that is more like an opening. I take a minute or two just to stand in relationship with those people and see what comes up for me to share from the silence about our time together. This closing isn't usually rollicking or dramatic, but it is heartfelt and in the spirit of what we've just been discussing. By the end of the talk, people understand and appreciate that.

Remember: Keep the Focus on Your Listeners

Kahlil Gibran said, "If [a speaker] is indeed wise, he does not bid you enter the house of his wisdom—but rather leads you to the threshold of your own."

The wisest approach to structuring your talk is not to overload it with your own brilliance and wisdom, but to present specific, easy-to-follow steps that listeners can use to get results.

You can put your talk together organically and effortlessly when you follow this simple structure. It leads your audience naturally through each of the steps they have to take in order to understand your message and make it real in their lives. And remember: whatever makes the talk more fun and satisfying *for you* will probably make it more fun and satisfying for your audience as well.

The next chapter shows you how to take the most important next step toward becoming an effective, inspiring, successful transformational speaker—at ease communicating in any arena. It is the secret to everything in this book.

. . . .

Chapter 13

YOUR PEER SUPPORT
SPEAKING CIRCLE

The best way to become a transformational speaker is to *practice,* and
the best place to practice is in a
Speaking Circle.

Though Facilitator Certification
Training is required for a person to
offer Speaking Circles commercially, no-fee peer support Speaking
Circles are encouraged.

There are hundreds of Speaking
Circles worldwide, some commercial, some peer support. Most of the
people interviewed for this book
first practiced transformational
speaking in one of these circles,
though some picked it up by reading
the first edition of this book.

Ellen Deck picked up the book to

"Attending a Speaking Circle is
like going to a great party and
spending quality time with the
most interesting people there."

•

"In the warm glow of soft available eyes I can see into my soul
with honesty and compassion,
and lovingly chip away all that
isn't me."

•

"The magnitude of being received
abundantly by eight people all
completely open to what you
have to say is enormous. It's like
recreating one's first life experiences in a rebuilt womb."

Speaking Circles is a service-marked brand name and may not be used to describe a
commercial offering without authorization by Speaking Circles International. See
Appendix A for information about the Facilitator Certification Training Program.

read on the long airplane flight from San Francisco to Florida for her parents' fiftieth wedding anniversary. At the party, she walked up in front of 125 guests to give a toast. In prior years she'd always had anxiety about speaking in front of people. But now she was not anxious at all!

"I took a deep breath, just like the book said. I took my time and felt the audience relax as I connected with them. This allowed my deep feelings for my parents to unfold and somehow shape themselves into words."

Liberated from a lifetime of trepidation around public speaking, Ellen began attending Speaking Circles back in the San Francisco Bay Area and is now a Certified Facilitator.

Creating Your Own Peer Support Speaking Circle

Will it help you along in this process to create a peer support Speaking Circle? A Speaking Circle is the ideal way to practice the art of Transformational Speaking. If you feel that this is something for you, here are the specifics for setting it up.

Start small. A group of three or more around the dinner table is a wonderful family ritual before a meal. Such a group around a conference table is an ideal team-building tool to get a business meeting started. Or introduce it as a fifteen-minute "game" while sitting around the living room with friends. Simply give each person two minutes of absolute attention (no note-taking, no distractions, please) to get current.

Any gathering designed to tap people into their Inner Speaker so they can speak transformationally runs on an energy that is free, nonpolluting, completely enlivening, and infinite. It's called *human support,* and it can bring out the latent superspeaker in everyone.

Each group has its own character, logistics, look, and "feel."

I believe eight people is as large as a peer support Speaking Circle should get. If there are more people, it lasts over $2^1/_2$ hours—and that's too long for most of us to stay fully engaged.

You may sit either in a circle or in rows, perhaps with a small riser or platform in front of the room. Some groups have a videotape camera set up in the back, operated by a participant, or by a facilitator who doesn't fully participate.

Each participant gets equal time as the center of attention—regardless of how much or how little they imagine they have to say. Everyone gives all speakers, whether they speak or not, unconditional support and positive acceptance—silently while the person is speaking and with positive comments during feedback time.

The people in the group don't talk among themselves during or between speakers, nor comment on the *content* of people's talks.

The Safest Room on Earth

The most important thing about a Speaking Circle session is that it is *safe.* Judgments, criticism, competition, and anything other than wholehearted support are left at the door. We all get to have our say, and to be supported. This safety, the foundation of such groups, is what allows people to relax into their essence.

"We learn to focus on what is *right* in people," says a motivational speaker. "You're in the riskiest situation possible—speaking in public—and you find out that you don't have to alter your basic self in order to survive. In fact, the more I'm *myself,* the better it turns out. That changed everything for me. It showed me I could trust myself just to relax and be wherever I am in my life!"

A psychologist says, "The safety lets us take risks, and that is where we find ourselves—in that risk-taking. That's where the magic happens, and where people blossom and unfold. An unexplainable presence gets activated when people come together as witnesses to one another in that safe environment."

Our truest selves come out when it is safe. When people were interviewed for this book, "safety" ranked highest on the list of what made people feel more spontaneous, creative, and confident.

When we get complete support for whatever we do, and whoever we are, we can drop our defenses and trust the group. That lets us stretch our limits while continuing to build on our strengths. When we see over and over that *we can be ourselves without anything bad happening,* we start to become more and more authentic. When the group's assumption is that we communicate well, we start to communicate even better.

Evie Belove, founder of the women's support group Celebrate Menopause, had always been externally oriented. Always looking around to see what was okay to say to this person, to this group, she tailored everything she said for her listeners. She says, "Transformational speaking has helped me to just be me and say whatever I have to say. It's like I can't make a mistake, and I suddenly feel expansive in my expression."

If you want something to grow, you put it in the sunshine. If *you* want to grow, put *yourself* in the sun of love and support. There aren't many places where people are safe today, but you can create one of them in your own living room.

A social worker told me she is patterning all her relationships after her peer support Speaking Circle. "It's an awesome experience to have total support without any criticism. If my husband and I have something to say to one another now, we say it in a loving and supportive way."

Positive Feedback

The only feedback in these sessions is concise and positive. Listeners don't give suggestions, critiques, advice, comments on the content of what was said—just brief comments about what they liked about spending time with the person up front. How did they experience his or her essence and connection with the group?

No matter where people begin, they make quantum leaps in self-expression when they receive generous appreciation and positive feedback, whereas the learning curve would plummet if shame were allowed to become part of the process.

As speakers, it's important that we really hear the positive feedback and take it in—for ourselves and for the people in the audience. They are giving us a gift, and it pains them when we refuse to receive it.

"In regular life we're taught to look for what's wrong," said a contractor. "We look for differences and things that bother us; we're not trained to accentuate the honest positive. Sometimes it's hard to receive honest praise, but if we don't, we do a disservice to ourselves and the others."

Just as miracles happen through positive feedback, I've seen very painful situations evolve when this guideline was ignored and people gave negative, or even neutral, feedback. I've also found that negative feedback is almost always highly inaccurate, and that it usually reflects an agenda on the part of the person who gives it.

One woman asked her Midwestern peer group of professional speakers to put the guideline aside "just this once" so that she could get some "realistic feedback" on what to do with one of her stories. They agreed, but the minute they started giving objective evaluation—nothing said was particularly negative—she fell apart. She understood immediately why this guideline is so important.

Receiving positive feedback lets us experience warmer and more trusting connections with others, and lets us witness the good in ourselves. And it opens up new levels of love and power—in front of the room, and in life.

Videotape is a good tool for confirming that the positive feedback you got was accurate, rather than the others just being nice. It also gives you an opportunity to see in private what you may want to change the next time, without hearing about it in public.

How It Works

Let's paint a picture of what a new circle looks like. We'll talk later about your role as the facilitator (if that's a role you choose), how to keep the circle safe, and how to handle your own and others' feedback. For now, we'll just look at the "what happens" part of the circle.

I once asked an extremely successful professional speaker and Speaking Circle veteran what he felt was the most important thing about starting a new circle. He told me, "Stick with the format, and keep it simple. Whether you think these things are good ideas, or you think you have a better way to do it—do it this way anyway. The whole well of *creativity* and *safety* come out of this specific format."

The standard circle has six to eight people, each taking three minutes in front of the group to "check in," then five minutes in the next round to speak about anything they want, with positive feedback. Use this format when you have a group of regulars who are committed to the process.

When you are first starting out, however, I suggest the following modified format.

Weaving the Circle

Begin with a group of three to six people who want to compel rapt attention every time they speak. They must be willing to support one another, and agree to follow precise guidelines during the session. These Standards of Support are listed later in this chapter. I suggest you read them aloud before you begin.

Arrange the chairs in a circle. The first time around, the group gives each person one minute of *silent support and attention*. (The volunteer facilitator acts as the timekeeper, and says, "Thank you" at the end of each person's turn.) The person who is the center of attention *does not speak*, but takes in the positive regard and silent appreciation of the group. He or she practices receiving support in silence, and maintaining soft eye connection with one person, then another and another. It's very important that there is *no conversation* at this point, even between people's turns.

Next, go around the circle again—this time for two minutes each. The person presenting takes in the attention and support, *free either to speak or not.* Although there should never be a formal topic, many people are moved to talk about a current life issue they are facing, a significant incident in their lives, how they are feeling about work or family, how they spent the morning, or what it's like to be the center of attention. Other people are moved at this point to stay silent and just *be* with the group.

When it is your turn to be the center of attention, *receive the support silently for at least a few seconds before speaking.* You do not have to speak at all. Your priority is to receive and feel the support for being yourself. Speak only when—and if—the spirit moves you.

If you do speak, speak directly to one listener at a time. *Pause* to "watch" your words sink in. Keep *eye contact* with individuals in the group, *one at a time,* rather than scanning the audience. Notice a tendency to avert your eyes or turn inward to figure out what to say next. Gently let go of that tendency to consult your inner Rolodex. Take in the support. Stay with people. Be willing to hang out in the unknown. Stop trying to "hold it together" or to be clever.

Let what you say come from your relationship with the group in the moment, not from memory or ideas you brought with you. *Allow silences,* and *let yourself be surprised* by what comes up. When you don't know what to say, stay with one person in the silence. There's no rush, and *speaking is not the priority.* The priority is to receive the support of the person with whom you are connecting. Ideally, you are connecting with someone or other in the audience 100 percent of the time.

"Dare to be boring" rather than chatter to cover anxiety. Remember that you are completely safe to feel the fear or the elation, the expansiveness or the shyness. The group has absolute patience and supports you completely no matter what you are feeling or saying.

When you are being an audience, you may be tempted to

think about what you're going to say when it's your turn. Gently let go of these thoughts. It's hard to give the speaker your complete attention and support when you're thinking about what you're going to say. Also, you'll miss the experience of letting just the right words come to you out of your relationship with the group when it's your turn. Allow what you say—or don't say—to come up naturally, rather than planning it.

Five Minutes of Bliss

By the time each person has had two turns (one minute in silence and two minutes either speaking or not speaking) following these guidelines, there will be a feeling of deep listening in the room. It is grace, or what some people call "ritual space." The group has become a community, and willingly remains quiet even between speakers.

Now each person takes five minutes to follow the thread of a feeling, thought, or idea. He or she may tell a story, discuss a challenge or stress, an obstacle, a joy, a sorrow, whatever emerges in this precious atmosphere of support. Again, *remember the option of remaining silent*. The person speaking also has the option of standing in front of the group or remaining seated.

As always, when it is your turn, *take in the silent support before you start*. Notice people, catch up with yourself. Explore something, perhaps for the first time. Something you haven't figured out. Find the answer as you speak, to get the "aha" in front of the room, or not. This is how you learn to "think on your feet."

You might tell a story from your life that is still "charged," and see if any new insights emerge. Or talk about your day.

Maybe you're facing a challenge or obstacle. See if some guidance comes out of the silent support. Some people use this time to sing or explore movement. The form of communication doesn't matter; it's all about *connecting*.

The volunteer facilitator signals by raising a finger when thirty seconds are left. The speaker finishes within that approximate time, and *takes the applause into his or her heart*. If you have resistance to taking in the applause, notice your tendency to cut it off. Then try to open up to it a bit. Practice taking it in, and this support will be reflected in other areas of your life and work.

After the speaker is finished, the facilitator asks the person to report briefly on his or her experience with the question, "How was that for you?" The speaker shares briefly how it felt to be in front of the room speaking in that way, then the facilitator invites comments from the group. People give brief, positive feedback. What did you like about the speaker? What positive feelings and values came through? *It is absolutely crucial that no one gives advice, "good ideas" for improvement, or comments on the content. We don't talk about the ideas, opinions, or story that people shared.* Only give your personal feelings about how it felt to be with that person as he or she stood in front of the room.

As the circle progresses and the room becomes increasingly "safe," people's sharing becomes more vulnerable. Hearts and souls open as people connect with and support one another. Laughter and tears frequently show up.

This all happens only to the extent that we are able to give up the urge to be clever, to entertain others, control the situation, "make something happen," or engage in cross talk, problem solving, or advice giving. Participants are learning to speak and to listen at a deeper level—as individuals and as a group.

The Next Level

. . . .

As the group develops purpose and continuity and plans a regular meeting schedule (every week or every other week is recommended), consider videotaping. You might also consider a microphone and amplifier, as well as moving from a circle to theater seating facing a small stage or riser—although you can start without any of these things.

Videotape adds a new level of magic, as speakers see how good they really are. After an occasional initial negative reaction ("Look at my hair!!" "I'm so fat!!"), people are amazed at how much better they look on tape than they felt when they were standing in front of the room. Watch your first tape at least three times to get beyond those critical voices. Listen to the positive feedback. Start to see the same beauty in yourself that others see, and that you see in them.

The active ingredients of total support and positive attention are addictive. As you become more effective as a speaker and realize you are speaking from the inside out, begin to *relish* your time in front of the room.

Start to feel the joy and satisfaction of your leadership role as you reach the hearts, minds, and souls of audiences with deep emotional impact, natural humor, and the charisma that comes from receiving and connecting with your audience.

Holding the Space: Your Job as Facilitator

. . . .

In a peer support Speaking Circle, one of the participants can double as facilitator, which can be a revolving position as people learn how to handle it. In this role, you model support, listening, and positive attention for the group. You are the person to whom people can look for complete acceptance and encouragement.

Here is a good description of what the facilitator does, in form and substance, as described by one:

> I'm just there to make it safe for everyone. To make sure people give the speaker their full attention, to have people really take in the applause after they speak, and to make sure all the feedback is positive, and that they talk about what they felt as people spoke. If I model those things, if I have a supportive, receiving, positive attitude, then the participants will do them, too.
>
> I'm not a teacher. When I play the role of facilitator, I'm the one who learns. I get to live in the light that people give off as more and more of their essence emerges. My job is to just get out of the way and let the evening come out of them. It's like ice-skating. Every person is different, and we all have to find our own edge on the skates. My job is to make it safe enough for them to experiment and find their edge.

Make the circle a "listening meditation" for yourself. Facilitator Charise Diamond says that a fringe benefit of being a facilitator is that her listening skills have improved and she is now a "peaceful listener." Through the practice and discipline of listening to speakers who expect positive honest feedback after their talk, she has learned to listen unconditionally without having to sort, classify, analyze, project, predict, censor, approve of, or disapprove any of it. "I can relax, knowing that the best feedback will surface on its own, like cream on milk." she says.

Hearts open as the speaker emerges and freely expands into the space created by the peaceful listener.

In the end, the circle is safe and powerful because we want it to be. By treating it as sacred—the space, each person, and the process—we make it *become* sacred. We see the essence of each individual, and watch each person blossom. We can make it safe even for the shyest people by talking about the beauty of vulnerability, of how we are all afraid. By respecting people, whatever they are going through, we help them respect themselves more. By our optimism, they notice their unique strengths. Expect them to succeed and they do.

Even if someone is slow to receive support, or they find it difficult to let go of an artificial style or "schtick," just be patient and supportive. Make the space even safer by encouraging them to be exactly who they are. Sooner or later they will come around, if they stick around.

When the facilitator gently signals that there are thirty seconds left in a person's turn, the signal means "thirty seconds more or less." The facilitator does not signal again unless the speaker goes on for at least one minute after the signal.

It is critical that each person has equal time in front of the room. Some may feel that what they have to say is so valuable they can keep talking well beyond the thirty-second signal. If this happens, remind them privately that the content of the talk or getting their problem aired is not the point; it's the *connection* that matters.

Holding people to their time limit is important because we are free to listen to and support a person completely *if we know when they're going to stop.* Outside these circles, people often talk for much longer than most others can tolerate. If we know someone will stop in five minutes, we are less likely to be inattentive or judgmental.

Suppose someone completely loses his or her connection with the group, or runs amok in some other way. It's never ideal to intervene when someone is in front of the room, because you're implicitly saying something is wrong. But sometimes I give a cue to "breathe" by connecting with them silently from where I'm running the videotape while taking a deep breath myself.

With speakers who do not keep their eyes available, I might signal by discreetly pointing to my eyes.

More rarely, I'll say "No rush" if someone is speeding forward and has lost the group. Or I'll just gesture with palms down to indicate, "Stay here with us. Stick with us." Sometimes I'll even say those things out loud. This is a very delicate issue and calls for good judgment as to when to intervene and when to let people continue in their struggle. Usually it's best not to intervene—but if your gut tells you to, do it gently, and be willing to back off if they resist you.

The "art" of being real can't be taught. Each person has to discover their own way. Support and trust them as they are, and just wait for the magic.

Setting Up the Circle

Let's say your peer support Speaking Circle has grown to eight regulars. Each person stands up in front now when it is their turn. Perhaps the group feels comfortable sitting in a semicircle, or likes theater-style seating, in two rows of four. Try both ways. Sometimes it's the shape and size of the room that determines which works better.

When you start the meeting, talk to people gently and conversationally from your heart about the safety of the room. Read and get agreement on the Standards of Support, the official guidelines to which each circle member needs to agree. You may copy and distribute them, and discuss them before you begin.

Standards of Support

A circle is as effective as the room is safe. For optimal safety and best results for all, we agree to maintain the following standards of support:

Confidentiality:

- We do not take content of talks outside of the circle, unless we have specific permission.

While a person is presenting, we as audience members, to the best of our ability:

- Maintain soft, positive focus on the face of speaker
- Remain quiet except for laughter if it comes up naturally
- Do not take notes or engage in any other distracting behavior
- Do not respond out loud, even if asked a question by speaker

*When giving feedback, we **do:***

- Keep it brief (no more than seconds) and clear
- Frame it absolutely in the positive
- Talk about *our own* feelings

*When giving feedback, **we do not:***

- Discuss content of the talk
- Talk about the speaker's life
- Evaluate or compare this talk with previous talks they've given
- Analyze, coach, or advise
- Turn attention to ourselves

When receiving feedback, we:

- Just receive the feedback into our heart the best we can
- Do not make comments to the people giving feedback, beyond "Thank you"

During breaks and after Circle:

- We are sensitive about initiating conversations with others based on the content of their talks. This includes good ideas, prying questions, and unsolicited advice.

Talk content:

- The only restriction on talk content is that it not reflect negatively on anyone present.

If you are unwilling or unable to maintain any of these Standards of Support, please bring it to the attention of the circle facilitator.

Find out if group members are willing to agree to these guidelines. If they are not, they are discouraged from attending. *The safety must be absolute.* Each participant has to make safety and support their number one priority.

If there comes a time when you no longer find it necessary to read the Standards of Support before every circle, at the very least remind everybody of the main principles:

- Everyone gives the speaker unconditional support and positive acceptance—silently while the person is speaking and with positive comments during feedback time.
- The speaker receives that support, letting in the attention, applause, and positive feedback from the group.
- We don't talk among ourselves during or between speakers, or comment on the content of people's talks (what was said, rather than how it was said).

Review the agenda for the group before each circle. Explain that we go around once so that everyone can stand in front of the room to "check in" for three minutes, with no feedback.

Then each person gets up and has five minutes to talk, connect in silence, or do whatever he or she wants with that time. This is followed by brief, positive feedback. (If video is used, each person brings a videotape each week, and the three-minute "check in," the five minutes, and the feedback are all taped.)

As the facilitator gives the introduction, he or she models the support and safety that are the foundation of these groups. No matter what is going on in the facilitator's own life, participants get 100 percent attention and positive regard. The facilitator takes the lead in looking for the best in each person, for the inner beauty and strength that are finding their way to the surface, and genuinely supports their emergence for each participant. After the ground rules and logistics are covered, the facilitator pauses before leaving the platform to accept the group's applause and goodwill.

Then one by one, each person gets three minutes in front of the room to check in, say hello, share where they are, and "get here." Some people "check in" in silence, slowly being with one person, then another, and another—receiving each person's support and acceptance. These three minutes are simply a chance to get present in the room.

Then we start around the circle again, and each of us has five minutes to do whatever we want: speak about something we've planned to discuss, talk about whatever pops into our heads, sing, talk about our lives, or stand in the silence. Whatever we do, or don't do, we get unconditional support and positive regard from the audience. At the end of five minutes, the facilitator asks us how it was for us, and then we get positive feedback from the group about what they felt and experienced while we were in front of the room.

After everyone has had their three minutes, their five minutes, and their feedback, the facilitator closes the meeting with a short wrap-up. With eight people, the circle takes about 2½ hours—and people usually spend a little time afterward catching up with one another, building friendship and community.

Essence Feedback: The Invisible Layer of Support

As the facilitator and the participants in your circle attune their feedback more and more to the *essence* of each speaker, an invisible layer of safety and support takes root.

This attuned positive feedback, and the layer of support it creates, is like the air we breathe—unnoticeable until there is a lack of it. When the feedback is attuned to the essence of the person, the air becomes pure and sweet and easy to breathe. When it is not attuned, the air starts to stagnate and the ease in the room begins to evaporate.

For the facilitator there is a vital importance in paying exquisite attention to the feedback. The more the facilitator can guide the feedback toward focusing on the essence of the speaker, rather than on content or advice, the safer and more powerful the experience will be for everyone in the room.

Positive, personal feedback is powerfully transformative for the person giving the feedback as well as for the speaker. To be able to give such attuned positive feedback, listeners must listen with all of their senses. In doing so, they become more sensitized to the speaker, as well as to themselves, awakening a sensitivity that expands the channels of their own creativity.

Giving this kind of feedback takes practice. But it is helpful to have a sense of what is meant by attuned positive feedback that relates to the essence of the speaker. Some examples and explanations are offered here for reference.

The most powerful feedback directly involves the experience of the speaker and the listener. Positive feedback conveys the *listener's* delight in the *speaker's* delight. It says, I am delighted in what has delighted you—what was important to you was important to me.

Examples from actual circles:

- "Your courage and truth moved me to tears."
- "You open me to very tender places."
- "I was inspired by your determination."
- "I felt honored that you shared your vulnerability."
- "I love your ruthless determination to get at your truth."
- "I felt your quiet resolve."
- "I had a sense of this precious flower being revealed."
- "Your authenticity made time stop for me."
- "Your eyes sparkled."
- "I loved the quality of fun as you wove that story."
- "It is amazing how you take something so simple and make it so profound."
- "I was lifted by the sweetness of your voice."
- "I appreciate your willingness to play out on the edge."
- "You awaken me to how precious life is."
- "I felt like I was watching a prayer."
- "I felt like the most precious person by being in your gaze."
- "You hit me like a firecracker of fun."
- "Your compassion strikes me like a clear bell."

Feedback that focuses on the *positive essence* of the speaker draws forth the real self. Feedback that focuses on *content* draws forth only a persona. Feedback directed to the essence of the speaker conveys the important message that it is *who you are,* not what you say, that is so engaging and precious.

It also says that it is safe to be whoever you are here: funny, sad, angry, poignant, boring, loving, passionate. And we will reflect who you are, with all your creative, passionate aspects, back to you.

Examples of content feedback, and how the facilitator might intervene:

- "When you talked about your mother's illness, I . . ." Facilitator says, "Sally, please let's keep away from content." Sally might say, "Okay. . . . I love the courage with which you talk about challenges in your life. It gives me a sense of hope dealing with *my* challenges." Facilitator: "Thank you, Sally."
- "I've also had a problem with weeds in my garden, and . . ." Facilitator interrupts: "Max, please keep your feedback to what you liked about being with Jim." Max might say, "You have a quality of earthiness that makes me want to plant myself in your garden."

Content-oriented feedback is often less succinct, pulling attention away from the speaker to the person giving the feedback, as well as calling attention to the story rather than to the person *telling* the story.

Many responses to the speaker can *seem* like positive essence feedback. Favorable comparisons to past presentations or encouragement to keep up the good work may feel supportive and may even be gratifying for the speaker to hear, but they are still a kind of a limit, and may place a subtle expectation on the speaker for future talks.

The intent here is not to be overly self-conscious. The kind of feedback I am encouraging is an art and a gift. Every circle is a work in progress, and it is the positive intent of the participants and facilitator that creates the first important layer of safety and support. This invisible layer begins to form as we climb to higher altitudes to see the larger vision of the person, so they can see and experience the larger vistas in themselves. With participation and practice, essence-attuned feedback becomes ever easier to give, and to receive.

The World of the Circle

Each time a circle meets, a new community is woven. The evening's themes flow into one another, and people become connected in new ways. The next time that circle meets, they begin from a place of deeper connection; as it continues to meet, the connecting continues to deepen.

In regions where there are many circles, such as the San Francisco Bay Area, people often attend more than one—and find a larger community of people who share the same experience and values. People from all over the country are starting to meet one another and recognize an even larger community.

As the transformational speaking community expands and becomes stronger, we shine our light on more and more people with whom we have contact. Whenever a new circle forms, the larger circle expands and our community grows stronger, wider, and deeper. We all become more committed to supporting one another, and to receiving support from others.

I am committed to making this work available to anyone who wants it. If I can support you in any way, please contact me at:

Lee Glickstein, Speaking Circles International
450 Taraval Street, #218, San Francisco, CA 94116
1–800–610–0169; e-mail: lee@glickstein.com;
Web site: www.speakingcircles.com

I picture each one of you in front of a circle of support, and send you my love.

End Note

. . . .

As I end this book, I'm happy for those of you who will read it. Because I know that when you use these simple ideas in the days just ahead, many of you will experience a warmth and joy, in your communications and in your life, that will seem close to a miracle.

Many people study transformational speaking specifically to grow psychologically, emotionally, and spiritually. Others wish to enhance their careers or improve their presentation, and are amazed that they also experience great personal growth. Change, growth, and personal evolution are inevitable results of these principles because we focus on being present, authentic, open, and connected with ourselves and others.

The world beats a path to the door of those who have applied their greatest gift to their biggest challenge. Transformational speakers unfold from the inside out. Unconditional acceptance heals their past and transforms their present, and this same magnificent power can evoke their *future,* pointing them toward their authentic livelihood—work or service that feeds their heart, nourishes their soul.

Recent developments that bear watching:

• Speaking Circles for adolescents are flourishing. The four elements that young participants find most challenging and rewarding are learning to make eye contact, learning to listen deeply to others, receiving acknowledgment (being appreciated), and learning how they *really* look and act by seeing themselves on videotape.

• Speaking Circles have helped people with ADD (Attention Deficit Disorder) by assisting them with listening, speaking, and self-esteem problems. One out of twenty people suffers from ADD. The symptoms include inattention, impulsivity, and, sometimes, motor hyperactivity. *The best antidote to attention deficit is massive doses of positive attention.*

• Speaking Circle participants are receiving relief from food, weight, and body image concerns. Most sufferers of eating disorders have low self-esteem and a distorted body image. In the presence of an unconditionally accepting audience, a person is free to discover her *real* self. This discovery can reveal the true nature of her conflicts, and make them available for resolution.

The author could not fully address all these areas in one book. The reader will be happy to know, however, that the simple, main principles of *Be Heard Now!* apply to many areas of life, including the one that means so much to us—the ability to speak with ease before audiences. And to be, at last, one's true self.

. . . .

CERTIFIED SPEAKING
CIRCLE FACILITATORS

◎

As of this book's publication date, more than eighty Speaking Circle Facilitators have been certified to lead Circles in the United States, Canada, and England. Speaking Circles International offers a wide range of programs including weekly 2¹/₂ hour and all-day Speaking Circles, three-day intensive retreats, facilitator certification training, and other advanced programs. Focused Circles include workshops for women, creative artists, clergy, storytellers, children, people with body image / eating issues, and more.

For information about Facilitator Certification and other Speaking Circles International programs, please see our Web site at www.speakingcircles.com, or contact:

- Executive Director, Jo Anne Smith, 800–610–0169 or 415–381–8044, circlesmith@earthlink.net
- Training Director, Doreen Hamilton, 510–524–4055, doreenhamilton@compuserve.com
- Training Director, John Potts, 925–837–8806, JohnRPotts@aol.com

• Founder, Lee Glickstein, lee@glickstein.com, Web site:www.glickstein.com

The following Facilitators have been trained and certified to conduct Speaking Circles according to the standards laid out in this book, and are authorized to offer Speaking Circles commercially.

CALIFORNIA (NORTHERN)

Alameda: Cathy Dana, 510–523–7853, Pollyanna4@aol.com
   Kim Soskin, 510–521–6523, ksoskin@gateway.net
Belvedere: Astrid Scott, 415–435–0203,
   ascott@sinewave.com
Berkeley: Jon Cotton, 510–653–3473,
   joncotton@post1.com
   Doreen Hamilton, 510–524–4055,
   doreenhamilton@compuserve.com
   Suzy Papanikolas, 510–540–5735
Concord: Ron Henry, 925–676–8651, rlhenry@silcon.com
Danville: John Potts, 925–837–8806, JohnRPotts@aol.com
Dillon Beach: Laurinda Gilmore Graves, 707–878–2544
Fairfax: Daniel Ellenberg, 415–457–7705,
   2relate@nbn.com
   Susan Thorsen, 415–258–1765, perfedge@aikido.com
Hayward: Sandi Jones, 510–581–3588
Kentfield: Bonnie Hoag, 415–485–1177
Mill Valley: Ellen Deck, 415–381–2367,
   CLAIRLIGHT@aol.com
   Kay Pepitone, 415–383–1593,
   kpepitone@marinternet.com
   David Roche, 415–383–3952, daveroche@aol.com
   Jo Anne Smith, 415–381–8044,
   circlesmith@earthlink.net

Morgan Hill: Skip Borst, 408–779–6469,
SkipBorst@Leadership-Coach.com

Novato: Michael J. Allen, 415–884–0625,
Healartma@aol.com

Karen Solomon, 510–339–7106, ksolomon@pacbell.net

Oakland: Barbara Druker, 510–653–6104,
BarbaraD@pacbell.net

Kim McCourt, 510–653–7944, kimmccourt@aol.com

Ease Oldham, 510–530–7849

Mary Owen, 510–271–0014

Palo Alto: Lisa Lewis, 800–436–2699

Lee Smith, 650–325–9077, lpsmith@aol.com

San Anselmo: Carol LaDue, 415–460–1701,
cladue4231@aol.com

San Francisco: Andrejka Coklyat, 415–750–3377,
andgraph@hotmail.com

Sara Hart, 415–357–9355, SaraHart@HARTCOM.com

Roland Jarka, 650–794–9955, rjarka@ix.netcom.com

Lauren Knoblauch, 415–835–4737, lrk@mindspring.com

Carol Payson, 415–821–5723

Cate Potyen, 415–273–1496, cpotyen@igc.org

Caterina Rando, 415–668–4535, CaterinaR@aol.com

San Jose: CJ Jensen, 408–338–4832, ImagingCJ@aol.com

San Leandro: Ron Gibbs, 510–895–1542,
rmgibbs@iname.com

San Mateo: John Harrison, 415–647–4700,
jcharr1234@aol.com

San Rafael: Lisa Hauck, 415–457–1357, lisamiso@aol.com

Jonathan Levy, 415–456–7461, jonkeithl@aol.com

Suzanne Malkin, 415–472–7997, SKMalkin@aol.com

Katherine Mapes-Resnik, 415–454–2674,
KATHMR@aol.com

Santa Rosa: Bob Fies, 707–545–2313, BobFies@ap.net
Tiburon: Lynne Shore, 415–435–4372

CALIFORNIA (SOUTHERN)

Carlsbad: Lynne Goldfarb, 760–804–9983, prana@aznet.net
San Diego: Barbara Goodman, 619–481–1554,
  barbara@begreat.com
San Luis Obispo: Kimberly Young, 805–466–5117,
  kyoung@tcsn.net
Santa Monica: Patricia Amrhein, 310–828–5588,
  patricia6@earthlink.net

COLORADO

Boulder: Mary Evitts, 303–494–5348
See also: Avis Ives, Texas; CJ Jensen, California (San Jose)

FLORIDA

Tampa: Ernesto Fernandez, 813–977–2832
  ernestojf@earthlink.net

IDAHO

Twin Falls: Wendell Edwards, 888–715–9555,
  wendell@actionalliance.com

NEVADA

Elko: Philip Blagg, 800–659–8055, x11288

NEW JERSEY

Montclair: Jeremy Nash, 973–233–0785,
  Jeremy_Nash@hotmail.com

NEW MEXICO

Santa Fe: Jeanne Silk, 800–715–3019, jsilk@earthlink.net

NEW YORK

Hyde Park: Carl Rohde, 914–229–8436,
  carlrohde@compuserve.com

PENNSYLVANIA

Pittsburgh: Marcia Clark, 724–941–3228,
  MCPresents@aol.com

TENNESSEE

Gatlinburg: Tina Alston, 800–467–0654,
  tinaalst@bellsouth.net
Nashville: Chris Olson, 615–460–7235

TEXAS

Farmers Branch: Avis Ives, 972–869–0304,
  avisives@compuserve.com

CANADA

Victoria, B.C.: Elizabeth Blackburn, 250–598–6262,
  onwords@direct.ca
Toronto, Ont.: Knowlton Shaw, 416–622–6580,
  charliesdad@msn.com

ENGLAND

Bath: Misha Carder, +44 1225 313531
  Barbara McGavin, +44 1225 401973,
  bjmcgavin@gifford.co.uk
Bournemouth: Julie Sheridan, +44 1202 422157
  Jan Slater, +44 1202 431394

. . . .

PEER SUPPORT SPEAKING CIRCLE,

KANSAS CITY

*Led by Jill Fredal, a ministerial student at Unity Village, a peer sup-
port Speaking Circle has been meeting twice a month in Kansas City
since 1996. To celebrate the completion of their first year of Circles,
participants devoted their opening three-minute talks to sharing
what they have gained from the work. This transcript is offered to support and inspire the formation of new peer support circles.*

LIDIA

For me this has been an extraordinary experience because it
has enabled me to do something real and true and deep for
myself. It's easy to talk about unconditional love but it's hard
to *do*, and for me, it's particularly hard to do it for *myself!* It's
easy for me to love others, but it's harder for me to be good to
myself.

I have given myself permission to come to this circle un-
prepared, in whatever state of mind I'm in, even if it's sad.
I've cried, I've laughed, I've been silly. I've done all kinds of
things that came from however I was feeling in that moment.

The powerful message to myself is that it's okay for me to truly be *wherever* I am.

It's one thing to say that, and another thing to come and do it in front of a group of people. And to get their unconditional regard and have that be okay. Very powerful. It's translated into my life in lots of ways, including at home. I don't censor myself and I'm a lot better at accepting everybody where they are, without feeling like I need to change or control it. That is a wonderful gift, because however anyone is, however I am, whatever the situation is, I can accept it and work with it.

It's a lot more than a head trip. I feel it in my heart and in my gut and it's something that belongs to me. It's a tool that I have that gives me a real sense of peace and power. I hope we do this for a very long time, because I cannot wait to see who I might be in another year! And I want to thank all of you for being there for me. [Applause]

BARBARA

This circle has been life-changing for me, and something for which I'm forever grateful. When we started, I had done just one speaking engagement in my life and did not feel good about it.

I echo what others have said about not being prepared and trusting that things would work out. Sometimes the most incredible things have come out of all of us. What I love about the group is that there seems to be an energy among us that we converge on, but we each have our own perspective. So it turns out to be an incredibly powerful evening and it flies by like *that!* [Snaps fingers]

The comfort and relaxation I have felt in standing in front of a group of understanding people has been incredible. I have come to get a sense of who I am as a speaker, what style I have. It may be different from other people's styles, and I can work on what I want to add. I've come to accept some of the parts that are just me naturally, even if they're different from others.

The way I've gotten to do this is to practice it here, then go home and watch my tape—three times—so that I really do hear the feedback and it can sink in. And I also get to look at myself and make whatever constructive self-criticism I want to, about what *I* want to work on the next time we get together.

What's really awesome for me is a public speech I gave, which I created by twice videotaping what came out of my mouth extemporaneously. That became the structure of the speech that I then embellished to fit into twelve minutes. I said exactly what I wanted it to say! If I had to sit down and *write* that speech, I would have agonized for I-don't-know-how-long, but this work has made it so natural that I was able to come up with most of the speech really easily. I am grateful for that.

And I'm using these skills in my coaching business. I was talking with a client about his presentations and told him that he needed the audience as much as they needed him. Therefore, I said, it would be helpful if he could stay in touch with what they were going through and relate to it. Which is what I learned standing here in front of you this year. So it's something I can share in my coaching business.

I'm forever grateful for that wonderful day we first got together, and for this group of people. Forever grateful. [Applause]

BEV

The speaking circle was my third attempt at learning to connect with an audience. One-on-one I relate rather easily, but
it became clear to me as I began giving more presentations
that I was not able to do that with groups. I was very much
into scripting and a lot of preparation. For two weeks before a
talk, I could think of nothing else. I overprepared because I
was afraid I would be speechless. And as all of you know, I'm
seldom ever speechless. [Laughter]

I had tried Toastmasters and benefited from that, in that I
gave regular presentations there. But the feedback began to
upset me because it wasn't meaningful. I knew it wasn't the
answer for me.

The second thing I tried was a class based on the concept
that the brain knows what to say if we just "go with the flow."
Sounded good, but that direction just made it worse for me. I
grew up in the '50s, very reserved, always trying to do the
right thing, trying to be the perfect little child for a very strict
father. In the spotlight, or in the presence of people who I be-
lieved were evaluating me, I would clench and be unable to
project who I am and what I wanted to say. The instruction
"go with the flow" was just another demand I couldn't live
up to.

When I finally discovered the unusual concept of Speaking
Circles, I immediately recognized its value, and I have thoroughly benefited from it. I'm over the hump. My real challenge now is, how do I keep from being so free and open that I
embarrass myself? [Laughter] Do you have a solution for that?
Because I think I have a rather loose tongue now. [Laughter]

In addition to all of the speaking advantages I've gained
from being in this circle, I've met a wonderful group of people who are each unique. Probably people I would not have

met otherwise. And it came at a time in my life when I was feeling somewhat isolated because I was in a career transition, and moving away from the people that I spent the last twenty years with because our interests had changed. So not only did I benefit from a speaker's perspective, I also gained a whole new group of friends, and that's been really wonderful! Thank you. [Applause]

MAUREEN

After the first time I tried it, I was able to use this tool in a presentation. I was able to go out and find myself really nervous in a situation and tell them, "Guys, I'm nervous. I'm going to take some moments of silence while I calm myself down." And the audience just sat there and waited for me! I thought, "This stuff really works. This is pretty cool."

I publish a newsletter about mentorship, and I realized that this is a good tool for mentors, so I did a write-up in my newsletter promoting the circle. Then, because I work with an organization called "Girls to Women," I decided that the circle would be a really good concept for adolescent girls, and I'm working that into our programming for 1998. Next week will be the first time we try this, and I'll report later on how it went.

I find that this tool has become a part of my life and of who I am. On a personal level, I've come out a lot more. I've danced up here in front of this group, and I've sung. I've been about as outlandish as I can get, and this comes across in all my presentations because I'm much more relaxed. While I do a presentation I am at ease about going off on a tangent, because I can be in that flow and I know I'm responding to whatever the audience is asking for, even though they haven't said a word!

It's a very powerful concept to stand up and just be yourself and do what you want with your hands, and stand still if you want to, or move it you want to.

This circle is a very important thing for me and I appreciate it. [Applause]

JILL

This circle has meant a ton to me. It has allowed me to grow in consciousness, and in my thinking. And it's also allowed me to grow up as a person, as a woman, as a minister. It's really helped me have a voice and allow myself to be heard and fully seen and to share my passion and what's in my heart.

I've gotten behind my power and have begun to own that I have things that I want to share with the world and things that I want to say, and to begin to trust myself that these things are valuable and important. And I can do it with clarity and you can support me.

So it's made a big difference for me, especially in ministerial school. When I started school this year, I told my fellow students how I wanted to be supported. I did not want to be evaluated in the traditional way. I wanted only positive feedback, positive regard. Some of them thought I couldn't handle the "real" feedback. But as they've grown with me, you would be amazed at the creativity that comes from them when they can share what is right about you.

And I've seen that in this group! You come up with the greatest ways to support me and each other in saying beautiful, wonderful things about what is true, and what is right about each one of us. It's powerful. I've had many people at school say, "You give the most wonderful feedback to people." They tell me I really get right to the heart of who they are. And it's because of here. It's because I've had time after time after time to practice seeing what's right and wonderful about each of you.

I've learned on a professional level to continue giving positive feedback to people. And the other thing that's happening for me is that I've had people share with me over and over again, saying, "You know, when you speak, you speak with such clarity and conviction and you're so willing to get out there and just say what's in your heart." And I can hear it!

So it's been great. Thank you. [Applause]

THE IMPACT OF SPEAKING CIRCLES

ON CHRONIC STUTTERING

BY DR. ROBERT PERRY

◎

Robert Perry, M.D., is a neuropathologist at Newcastle General Hospital in England, and a lifetime stutterer / stammerer. (Note: "Stammer," as used in England, and "stutter," as used in the United States, are synonymous.)

It was evening in the hospital lecture theater. I stood "in the void" in front of the group at an introductory Speaking Circle. I breathed. I breathed again. I breathed yet again. I said nothing. There was no need to. Absolutely no need to say a word. But I was there, it was real, it was an audience in front of me. I was looking at them. I was in contact with them, yet I didn't feel uncomfortable or embarrassed, I didn't even feel a need to communicate. I didn't feel a need to speak. All I was doing was looking at individuals in front of me. And they were supporting me. And I was receiving that support. And that was all.

I could continue this for two minutes, for five, for ten or more minutes—it would make no difference. It was a different world. I was in a new and curious environment that made no demands, posed no threats, and only offered support. I stood and savored its splendor. I re-savored its apparent uniqueness. And as I stood on my feet, in front of this audience, I began to speak.

I breathed in and I told them my thoughts and feelings. "This is like a child in infancy," I said. "They gaze at their parents and absorb support and love. No demands are made. Yet a relationship is made and established in an intense, supportive, and—for parents and children—loving way that lasts a lifetime. Human contact at a very basic level, long since forgotten by the adult, long since superseded by learned cognition, behavior, and perceptions, but human contact at its most trusting and primeval best."

I again stood and reflected on what opportunities lay in this, to me, unexplored territory of direct, in-touch, human relationships. I realized it was unfettered by learned behavior. Unfettered by constraints, criticisms, suggestions, ideals, orders, promises, encouragements, discouragements, threats, or flattery. These and a million other perceptions and reactions had been acquired during infancy, childhood, and beyond—and memorized for instant access.

In that unique hypnotrance-like state of infancy, the human brain begins to absorb information, the child lies there and absorbs, and continues to absorb, absorbs at a rate that staggers belief. And establishes interactive memory banks that reflect the individual's character and personality. Most such information is essential. It is all unique to the child. Almost all beneficial. But perhaps for some individuals, a tiny percentage of this information, a tiny fraction relating to acquired habits and perceptions in the complex world of interhuman relationships, some information gets a little distorted, processed and stored a little askew.

And, and, and, and, and lead to a, a, a, a, hu, hu hes, hesit, hesitancy, a misperception of the loving environment and initially supportive human world. An uncertainty that grows. That grows and expands. And may remain. And may remain and replicate. And may remain, replicate, persist, torture, engulf, and imprison.

Stuttering. Stu sssssss, stu stu stu stutt, stuttttttering, ssstuttering, stuttering—to be more precise. Did you get that? I'll say it again, "stuttering to be more pre pre prec precise." Or should it be "Sta, sssssss, sta sta sta stamm, stammmmering, stammering"? Hell! We can't even agree on the name of the prison we're in. But we're in it all right. Its glass walls limit freedom—yet are imperceptible and unknown to the observer.

It may be self-imposed, but the barriers are as real as prison walls, and the more distressing for being invisible to the stutterer and the observer. This state seems real enough, but reality supervenes: Where am I now? I'm in front of this audience. (Do I remember past audiences? Do I remember past terrors, past memories—all too painful to recall now, shut away, locked, bolted, never consciously visited. And is this real, and is my name Robert, and is it spelled with one *r*, or two, or three?)

Where am I now? I'm in front of the same audience. And there is no need to speak! There is no pressure to perform! The world has changed for a moment. So let me think. . . . I'm in front of this audience . . . and, and being in front of an audience doesn't matter! It doesn't matter any more! There is no pressure, no anxiety, no apprehension, no concern. The immediate situation has new ground rules. My perceptions have changed, and in doing so they transport and transform me. I realize I have returned to a world long since forgotten,

forgotten but now very real, that assumes no preconceived ideas, actions, or reactions, but exists as an environment that can, in a benign but powerful way, be used to reset an individual's perceptions, emotions, and beliefs.

And for the stutterer, to reestablish self-belief, self-respect, communication, and communication skills. In a brief and imperceptible interlude, I had entered a magic land. I said, "Hello." I smiled. I had entered the world of Speaking Circles.

The Journey to Speaking Circles

My journey commenced with a trip to Amsterdam in December 1995 to see David McGuire, a recovered chronic stammerer who adapted the del Ferro diaphragmatic breathing technique. McGuire had added aspects of Joseph Sheehan's non-avoidance psychology and voluntary stammering, and allied this to a combative "sports psychology" to produce a robust method for breaking the back of stammering.

I had been encouraged to go to Amsterdam by fellow members of the Newcastle self-help group. The McGuire Program included unlimited contact with others who had been on his course, by telephone or at meetings, and a list of supportive books and articles. The latter included John Harrison's book *Conquer Your Fears of Speaking Before People,* published by the National Stuttering Project of California. This book details both practical and psychological aspects of stammering (Harrison's "Hexagon" of the interaction of physiology, emotions, behavior, beliefs, intentions, and perceptions). At a workshop in London in 1996, Harrison described "Speaking Circles" and how useful they are.

In my view, recovering from stammering is not a single,

simple process. It can be likened to visiting an art gallery over a period, and studying many pictures on a long wall. These pictures are not all in the same style, are not all on the same subject, are not necessarily painted by the same artist, and may not even appear to be connected or relevant to each other. Their overall theme, however, can be interpreted as "Recovering from Stammering."

The pictures on this wall include behavioral (especially breathing) techniques; non-avoidance psychology; cognitive psychology; support mechanisms; a willingness to practice; contact with other recovering stammerers (speaking pals); assertive techniques; how to achieve and maintain change; how to avoid relapse; an acquaintance with themes and ideas current in "paperback psychology" over the last decade or two; and attending speaking clubs such as Toastmasters and Speaking Circles. David McGuire has detailed many of these aspects in his book *Freedom's Road*.

The Speaking Circles Environment

Going to Speaking Circles is a powerful way of continuing and maintaining the recovery processes. At a Speaking Circle meeting, one has the opportunity to stand in front of the whole group, and speak—if you want to. But it is an equally effective process as an audience participant. In supporting the person out in front, the audience members listen, observe, and assimilate many of the basic elements necessary for natural, unstressed, group relationships and interpersonal communication skills.

The Speaking Circle environment is sheltered. It needs to be so. But it is beneficial to both the stutterer and the nonstutterer. How long it will take to show benefit in the outside world varies from person to person. It may take up to a year to see the benefit of regularly going to meetings in all non-Circle situations, but many situations will transform sooner. Maybe instantly.

My wife breezed in as an observer for half a Circle meeting and watched the process, while waiting for a lift home. She was lecturing the next morning. When we met up after her lecture she said, "You know, I tried that technique, I tried looking at the individuals in the audience in that lecture I gave, it transformed the situation. I felt at ease. I felt as if I could talk forever."

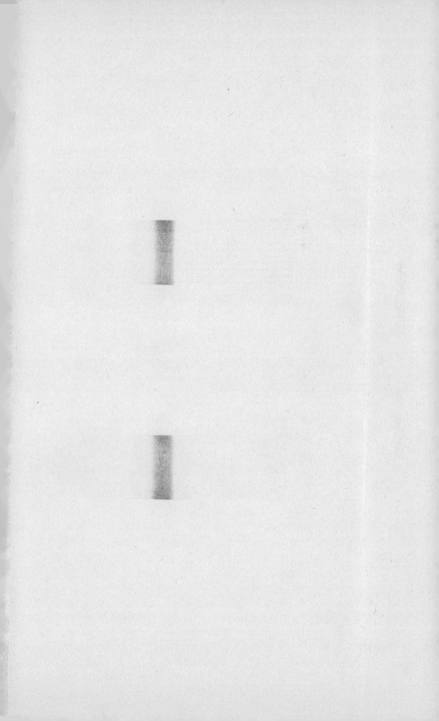